Studies in Political Science

Edited by DR MALCOLM ANDERSON
University of Warwick

6
OPINIONS, PUBLICS AND PRESSURE GROUPS
An Essay on *Vox Populi* and Representative Government

P.92 - 9 - good little history (handwritten annotation)

OPINIONS, PUBLICS AND PRESSURE GROUPS

An Essay on *Vox Populi* and Representative Government

Graeme C. Moodie
Professor of Politics, University of York

AND

Gerald Studdert-Kennedy
Lecturer in Politics, University of York

London
GEORGE ALLEN AND UNWIN LTD
RUSKIN HOUSE · MUSEUM STREET

FIRST PUBLISHED IN 1970

© *George Allen & Unwin Ltd, 1970*

ISBN 0 04 322001 0 *cased*
 0 04 322002 9 *paper*

PRINTED IN GREAT BRITAIN
in 10 point Plantin type
BY W & J MACKAY & CO LTD CHATHAM KENT

FOREWORD

Academia is all too frequently rent by sterile disputes. A current example is that between the advocates of 'behavioralism' (the American spelling is deliberate) and the defenders of 'political theory'. Neither require serious advocacy or defence; the only issue worth debate is the relationship between empirical evidence and evaluative judgment. To that debate we hope this book is relevant, in the sense that one of its main purposes is to try to relate both levels of discussion to one another. Only thus, we feel, can one attempt meaningfully to explore those basic themes of rationality and representation which are our central concerns.

We discuss them in the context of British politics, with further illustrations from the experience of the United States. In particular, we do so with reference to the most recent published research into the British political process. An incidental result is that the bulk of our material relates to British politics in the 1950s and early 1960s; but nothing has yet happened to suggest that the events of that period are eccentric or atypical. In any case our main purpose is to explore concepts and relationships which are more enduring than their current manifestations or application.

This book is the product of experience and conviction. The experience is that of teaching—and especially of jointly teaching a course here entitled 'Vox Populi'. The conviction is that a radical democratic commitment is neither irrelevant nor outdated. From these follow certain debts which we would like to acknowledge. For our experience we would like to thank our students at the University of York and elsewhere, as well as the colleagues, friends, teachers, and authors from whom, too, we have learnt. We also wish to thank those individuals in authority who, by their shortcomings, have refuelled our conviction. We can name neither group: the first is too large; the second is small enough to make elaboration defamatory. We also wish to thank Mrs Ray Nixon and Mrs Miller for their expert and speedy typing.

University of York   G.C.M.
December 1969   G.S-K.

CONTENTS

I

Politics and Democracy

Any group, any collection of two or more people, if it is to survive, will on occasion have to agree on common action and to decide, in common, which situations or issues require common action and which do not. Failing such agreement the group is likely to disintegrate or be destroyed. But not even in the most harmonious and loving of voluntary groups—an ideal marriage, for example—can such agreement be assumed always to exist without directing some activity or attention to securing it. Habit and mutual understanding will take the group a long way, but faced with any change in the environment or any other new situation agreement will have to be *reached*. In the ideal marriage envisaged, it may be easy to reach agreement, but in most groups it may not be possible always to build on 'natural' harmony, and in some it may be very difficult indeed, given the members' differing aims, tastes, perspectives and interests (i.e. their humanity). Difficult or easy, agreement may be essential: the children must go to some school, however deeply the parents are divided about private and public, selective and comprehensive schools; the rambling club must ramble somewhere, however much some members prefer the wolds to the dales; and to take the starkest example, the two owner-riders of a tandem bicycle must travel *together*, however much they disagree about the route. In each case they must all agree, or dissolve, and in each group there must be some process, some activity, whereby the arguments and conflicts are resolved. That process or activity is what we mean by 'politics'.

In its simplest form the human predicament which gives birth to the activity of politics is this: the members of a group face a situation which demands a common response, but disagree as to what the response should be. All are aware, however, that the response must be common, i.e. must be made or accepted by all members, including those who may have opposed it. Furthermore, the debate is predicated upon either the need or the desire for the continuance of the group (there is no problem if members can duck the issue of common action merely by ending their membership—an option which is, in fact, surprisingly rare or difficult to exercise).[1]

Not all disagreements need give rise to politics. Relevant are those only which relate to necessary common action, to those matters which come within the realm of the group's common, or public, affairs (the definition of which is obviously part of the public realm). For it is only in public affairs that competing policies (i.e. principles of action) have the distinctive characteristics of being binding on the group as a whole once adopted and thus of being mutually exclusive: the riders of a 'tandem' cannot simultaneously take the right- and left-hand forks; the Church of England cannot be both Established and disestablished. The essence of the political problem is that while one may succeed in having the best (or worst) of both worlds, yet it is never possible to have all of both worlds.

As a group survives, its political activities tend to follow regular, known, and predictable lines, to acquire a pattern. And depending upon how decisions about the group's public affairs are customarily taken, so the pattern may be labelled as autocratic, democratic, oligarchic or whatever else may be appropriate. In principle, moreover, political labels may be attached to any and every human group since, according to the view being put forward, politics is an inescapable attribute of all human groups; to all social life there is a political dimension.[2] It may not, of course, be the most important dimension in all cases, nor may a group's political patterns be its most distinctive feature, but the quality of life within any group is always, at least in part, a function of its politics.

Politics, we have said, is a dimension of all social units, but not all units are equally significant in terms of the decisions to be taken, or, putting it another way, of the centrality of their public affairs to the quality of existence. For most people it is still the case that the nation-state is the most important unit to which they belong. It is the state, and not the city, church, industry, or trade union, which is the ultimate guarantor of the fundamental order on which any meaningful life depends and which, therefore, is entrusted with the power to maintain it and, usually, the right to make those decisions believed to be necessary to define (or redefine) it. Above all, of course, the modern state is so large a social unit, involving such a complex differentiation of social roles and functions, that it is inevitable that there should also have developed an elaborate division of labour in attending to the unit's public affairs and political processes. It is true even of the most democratic

[1] This analysis of politics derives from S. E. Finer, 'The Study of Politics', *The University Quarterly*, Nov. 1953. He, however, does not stress, as we believe it essential to do, the constraints of group continuance.

[2] To talk, for example, of 'office politics' is not merely to speak metaphorically.

political systems yet known that some members of the society play a more active and public part than others in the decision-making process. Whatever the patterns, certain features are common to all political processes—more or less open articulation of different viewpoints on public affairs; more or less restricted (both in respect to what is said and who may say it) participation in discussing these viewpoints; more or less successful or legitimate attempts to persuade, coerce or silence those who disagree; and some recognized patterns or structures for conducting these activities, taking 'official' decisions on behalf of the unit concerned and trying to implement or apply those decisions. In all these respects social groups and units will vary immensely—from, for example, the patterns associated with Nazi Germany to those of the Society of Friends —but universal is the need to secure common action on public affairs by members who differ, or are liable to differ, in their preferences, interests and perspectives. The larger and more complex the unit, moreover, the more complicated and elaborate are the political patterns likely to be and the more difficult to label, let alone to describe or understand.

In this book we will primarily be concerned with trying to understand certain aspects of political processes, especially those which, like the British and American, claim usually to merit the label of 'democratic'. One of our purposes will be to examine this claim. But what, first of all, does it mean to claim that a political system is 'democratic'?

At the level of principle democracy, as we intend the concept, is three-dimensional, the dimensions being those of discussion, power and security. It is, to offer a minimal definition, a system of government in which decisions arise from a process of discussion, in which power is evenly and widely enough distributed for no single group or section within the polity to be able continuously and without challenge to exercise preponderant power, and in which each individual is secure enough from arbitrary external control, by private or governmental agencies, to be able freely to participate in the process of discussion and fearlessly to use the political resources at his command. This is not the place to offer a full defence of this definition, but some explanation and justification is obviously necessary. Let us examine the three 'dimensions' in turn.

1. *Discussion*. Much of the rhetoric of democracy, and many of its most characteristic institutions, are rooted in the notion of government by or after discussion. 'Ballots, not bullets', the central roles of assemblies and parliaments (places to talk), free speech, the 'market-place of ideas', and the 'open society' are obvious examples. The view that discussion, and not violence or other forms of coercion, is the distinctive method of democratic government (not that any form of government can totally dispense with coercion) derives from the liberal democrat's conviction

that no man or group of men *know*, with absolute and exclusive certainty, the answers to all human problems. All thought and action must therefore be open to criticism; and especially must those in power be criticized for the sake of efficiency, acceptability, and the avoidance of rigid orthodoxies. Among free and equal men argument and persuasion are, in the last analysis, the only appropriate means to secure both change and the agreed decisions on which social cohesion may depend.[1]

2. *Power.* At first sight the power dimension—the 'populist' emphasis upon the people as the source of authority and the ultimate decision-makers—may seem to have little connection with, even to be opposed to, the civilized vision of government by discussion. 'Government by the people' (the root meaning of 'democracy' after all) is to many only slightly less frightening than phrases like 'all power to the people' or 'the dictatorship of the proletariat' which conjure up pictures of bloodthirsty revolutionary mobs or the ruthless collective tyranny of a bogus majority will. That, on occasion, popular government may amount to this cannot be denied. Nevertheless, a theory or definition which totally excludes all reference to the central inspiration of self-government, to the ideal of universal citizenship, has nothing to do with democracy as it has always been understood. The point is that, while government by discussion amongst a circumscribed elite may be preferable to an elitist rule of some other kind, yet for it to constitute democracy, *all* the people must be given at least the opportunity to take part in the debate. If, moreover, the case for discussion rests to some degree upon the denial of all human claims to a monopoly of truth, then to deny to any sane adult the right to join is arbitrary and unjustifiable.[2] And the only way to ensure that 'ordinary people' will be accorded this participatory right is to back it with popular power—otherwise the unprivileged, the unwealthy, and the prestigeless will for ever also be the exploited, the dispossessed and the unheeded.

There is another reason why a democratic process of discussion requires a substantial sharing of power. One cannot talk of a genuine discussion unless all the participants accord one another a genuine hearing—a discussion is not a one-way process. This is to say that they must all regard the others with a sufficient degree of esteem and respect to

---

[1] On this dimension, see, in particular, A. D. Lindsay, *The Essentials of Democracy* (Oxford University Press, 1929 and 1935), and Bertrand Russell, *Philosophy and Politics* (Cambridge University Press for NBL, 1947). On the general topic of liberal democracy, see G. Sartori, *Democratic Theory* (Praeger, 1965).

[2] Unjustifiable in terms of the first dimension, that is. We are, of course, well aware that there are problems about the use of such words as 'sane' and 'adult' and we would in fact insist that the voice of many non-adults must be heeded. But these problems do not affect the general argument.

listen as well as to talk or give orders. It is rare, however, at least in political and public life, for men to listen seriously and comprehendingly to those who are in a position of continuing and marked inferiority of status and power. In a democracy, not only must the exercise of power (even by a majority) be guided and tempered by the rules and processes of discussion, but, it follows from what has just been said, preponderant power must ultimately inhere only in the generality of its members.

3. *Security*. The kind of security we have in mind is not merely or even primarily security against the effects of social misfortunes like sickness, old-age and maternity, desirable as it is. Rather it is that security against injustice and the arbitrary exercise of power which, in traditional liberal doctrine, is attained through the rule of law and the defence of such individual 'rights' as life, liberty and property. In saying this we are not unmindful of the objections which have been made to particular theories of rights and particular formulations of the rule of law. It must also be admitted that the liberal tradition has at times been unduly concerned with security against state power (and not enough with the dangers of and from 'private' organizations) just as it may have been insensitive to that aspect of 'property' which consists solely in being legally protected.[1] Nevertheless, the liberal insistence upon the need to defend man's life, livelihood and dignity against avoidable human deprivations is not dependent for its value upon the arguments of (say) Dicey or Locke. The fact remains that unless individuals are secure against such personal dangers their share in popular power may be worthless and their 'right' to participate in public discussion as meaningful as the 'right' to vote 'yes' in a Nazi plebiscite. If discussion be an 'essential of democracy',[2] it in turn is dependent for its reality upon the diffusion of power and the existence of the rule of law, each of which are mutually dependent in sustaining a system of democratic government.[3]

Even in such a brief and highly general discussion of democratic principles, it is not possible to avoid making some reference to actual political structures and processes, if only to illustrate our meaning. It is even less possible to do so as we become less abstract and move on to look at two other key concepts, both of which are more commonly

[1] That any job may be a form of property no less, and possibly more, sacred than real estate is only now being tacitly accepted in the spread of schemes for 'redundancy' payments below the 'golden handshake' level.

[2] See footnote 1 on page 14 above.

[3] It is arguable, however, that the rule of law is historically prior, in that it alone provides the governmental environment in which popular power can grow and new ideas spread. Perhaps there is a moral here for those countries which, as yet, only aspire to democracy.

articulated characteristics of democracy: representation and legitimate opposition.[1]

If one accepts the fact that, in any modern state, there must continue to be some division of labour between those who hold formal governing positions and those who do not, even if one does not take the further step of equating this distinction with that between the ruler and the ruled or the elite and the mass (a step which is by no means logically necessary), then it follows that any functioning democratic system must incorporate and rest upon a system of representation. This is to say that the formal 'governors' must 'represent' the other members of the society in the sense that they act, to quote Hanna Pitkin, 'in the interest of the represented, in a manner responsive to them. The representative must act independently. . . . The represented must also be (conceived as) capable of independent action and judgement. . . . The representative must act in such a way that there is no conflict (with those represented) or if it occurs an explanation is called for.'[2] This relationship of representation is essential to democracy in order to lend concreteness to the notion of participation, but, it must also be pointed out, the represented must include all adults if the populist principle is also to be respected. If, furthermore, the representative relationship is to be more than empty symbolism, then the system must provide for widespread and public discussion; for, otherwise, it would be impossible for the representatives either to be responsive to the interests of others or to offer explanations of their own behaviour.

Opposition appears less frequently than representation in the literature and rhetoric of democracy, for all the frequency with which books on British government sing the glories of its official (Her Majesty's) Opposition. Nevertheless, if only in the guise of criticism or dissent, it is generally recognized as a vital element in the liberal idea of democracy, and rightly so if governments (however representative) are denied the monopoly of truth. It is important to emphasize, however, and especially in a British context, that the idea of opposition must not be limited to and need not even include a single organized group or party as formal competition with the Government. The essential point is simply that those in government and those who support them may legitimately and publicly be opposed, criticized and even resisted subject, in effect, only (or primarily) to procedural limits and restraints.[3]

[1] On these concepts see, in particular, H. F. Pitkin, *The Concept of Representation* (University of California Press, 1967), and R. A. Dahl. (ed.), *Political Opposition in Western Democracies* (Yale University Press, 1966 and 1968).

[2] Pitkin, op. cit., p. 209.

[3] The qualification is, clearly, an immense simplification of the problems of obedience, disobedience and resistance in a democratic system. But, for present purposes, the simplification will suffice, provided only that one remembers that *all* principles are liable to conflict, that all principles must provide some indica-

Both concepts, it may be granted, are important to the specification and understanding of democracy; but neither is simple or self-explanatory. Numerous questions immediately arise about both concepts: what qualities or features of the represented should the representatives represent, and in what proportions? How can they be ensured? Within what limits, if any, may the representative act independently? To what extent must a representative perform a creative function? Is opposition to the system legitimate, or only to particular measures, policies or governors? What methods of opposition, if any, are illegitimate or harmful? Under what exceptional circumstances ought different answers to be given to the two previous questions? To what extent are the intensity and the variety of support and opposition the primary factors which must be represented in government? These are but some of the questions which may be raised. There are other, more specific ones, which need to be answered if one is to assess the significance of representation and opposition within any given political system. They relate, above all, to the established, institutionalized, structures and processes through which citizens oppose and are represented: the methods of selection, rejection and control of representatives; the resources available to those in opposition; the precise points within the decision-making process at which opposition or criticism is encouraged or discouraged, facilitated or made difficult; the groups, interests and ideas which, in fact, seem to secure strong or weak representation within the various political and governmental structures; the extent to which, and the policy areas within which, different opposition interests and viewpoints are so carefully heeded as to constitute, in fact, major governing influences or are virtually excluded from the formal structures and processes of government.

To many of these particular questions we will return.[1] The point we wish to make now is that fully to understand what representation or opposition means in a given context involves extensive empirical illustration. More than this, any attempt to define or explain the concepts themselves will inevitably be coloured by one's experience of representative institutions and of historical opposition. This is, of course, only to make a particular application of a general proposition about conceived purposes and their social manifestation: that the relationship is dialectical. Statements of purpose, or conceptualized goals, derive at least some of their meaning from institutions which seem to further them, but in turn the institutions will be operated and understood at least partly in terms of the purposes they fulfil.

---

tion of the circumstances in which they may be transcended, and that neither proviso undermines an otherwise valid principle.

[1] The primary emphasis, however, will be on those pertaining to representation.

For many people, for example, 'democracy' will be defined ostensively rather than by reference to certain principles or ideals. For them democracy means a system of government which centres upon such institutions as elections, control of an executive by a representative assembly, competing political parties, and an independent judiciary. Notably, as a matter of history, these institutions did not develop initially in order to establish 'democracy' in Britain (or England) but in answer to successive problems of a more immediate and varying kind: more effectively to control the monarch, to obtain more secure tax-revenues, to defend or advance particular interests, and so on. Nevertheless, they provided at least some of the inspiration, and much of the specific content, for the articulation of an ideal of democracy which, in turn, came to be used as a criterion for the operation, reform and, in some cases, rejection of those institutions. Hanna Pitkin concludes her study of representation by pointing out that 'the concept . . . is a continuing tension between ideal and achievement'.[1] This is as true of democracy.

The tension within the idea of democracy is very apparent today. Within what might be called the professional literature of politics the tension manifests itself most consistently in critiques or revisions of the traditional ideal in the light of its application. Numerous studies of voters and public opinion in Britain, the USA and elsewhere may be cited[2] in (at least partial) support of the view that the mass of people are too ignorant, apathetic and irrational both to fulfil the role of participant citizen and to translate the purpose of democracy into a tolerably effective and civilized form of government. In fact, as this line of argument admits, no country's system is fully democratic in the traditional liberal sense; that sense, it might seem to follow, is therefore to be regarded as utopian. Any meaningful democratic ideal, today, must therefore be redefined as consisting only of pluralism (for example, of the legitimate existence of competing elites linked to the masses by various intermediate groups and organizations)[3] or even of the occasional choice, by a mass electorate, between organized alternate political parties over the leadership and policies of which the electorate has little control.[4]

[1] H. Pitkin, Op. cit., p. 240.

[2] See, to name but two examples, D. Butler and D. Stokes, *Political Change in Britain* (Macmillan, 1969), and Angus Campbell and others, *The American Voter* (Wiley, 1960).

[3] Crudely to paraphrase the argument in W. Kornhauser, *The Politics of Mass Society* (Routledge & Kegan Paul, 1960). See also, for other variants, D. B. Truman, *The Governmental Process* (Knopf, 1951) and S. M. Lipset, *Political Man* (Doubleday, 1960).

[4] See J. Schumpeter, *Socialism Capitalism and Democracy* (Allen & Unwin, 1965), pp. 269 et seq., for the baldest statement of this attenuated democratic ideal.

On the other hand the later 1960s have seen, at the 'barricade' level, a recrudescent radical critique of the institutions of democracy in terms of the ideal, and in particular of the populist participant dimension thereof. This aspect of the tension, it is probably unnecessary to say, has become particularly closely associated with the waves of student unrest which have spared few countries throughout the world, regardless of the kind of 'democracy' for which they stand. Less dramatically, the movement for parliamentary reform in Britain, a movement supported mainly by academics and back-bench politicians, provides another illustration of the potentially solvent quality of a purpose when applied seriously to the institutions which claim already to embody it.

We hope that our discussion of the political attitudes and activities of the public, with particular reference to voting, public opinion and pressure groups, will contribute to the articulation and elucidation of this tension between democratic purpose and performance.

2

The General Public

Democratic theory and the 'evidence'.

Classical political theory has been preoccupied with two over-arching problems; the stability and survival of political systems and the rationality of political acts. Rational decisions, it has been assumed, lead to stable and successful government. The first rule of nature is to make peace, Hobbes pointed out, and it is human reason that devises means for doing this.

All the arguments, of course, have hung on the definition of rationality, and more particularly on the question of *who* in practice is to define what is rational or contribute to such a definition. The ultimate objective of the philosophers has been the 'good of the whole community', so the question has always resolved itself into establishing criteria for deciding which category or categories of person, under which set of rules or restraints, are most likely to make rational contributions to political decision-making for the good of the whole society. A large vocabulary of concepts—sovereignty, general will, obligation, citizenship, rights and so on—has been developed to provide theoretically satisfactory answers to this question.

The development of techniques for the systematic collection of data about public opinion seems to have added a new and troubling dimension to these familiar arguments. We are sometimes warned that this constant testing of public opinion might entail the development of a form of instant democracy, that would at best be vulgar, but which could also be disastrous for much that is valuable in our civilization. It is feared that politicians will learn to respond to the whims of irrational majorities and that an interfering and small-minded populism will undermine and confuse the various institutions that force decision-makers to engage in a process of deliberation over conflicting demands and over the short and long-term limitations on the resources needed to satisfy those demands.

This anxiety may be naive, but there are other anxieties that relate less to the possible misuse of opinion polls by the politicians, than to the implications of some of the material the polls have uncovered in supposedly democratic societies for the assumptions on which it is thought that democracies are based. Here, for example, are some representative survey findings. Three surveys in West Germany between 1958 and 1962 asked if people knew what the Bundesrat was. More than half said they did not. Another third gave answers that were vague or simply wrong. About 12 per cent got it right. It has repeatedly been shown that in any given year barely half the American population can name even one Senator from their own State. In Sweden in 1944, when asked, 'Do you remember anything that has happened in Parliament this spring?' 81 per cent could remember nothing. In France in 1954 almost half the men questioned in one survey claimed that they voted not on an issue but simply out of loyalty to party or to some general slogan. In 1960, a British sample was asked to differentiate between the two major parties in terms of 16 *party* goals or traits. On only 4 of the statements did as many as two-thirds of the sample attribute a clear-cut goal to either party, and these differences were not stated in terms of policy but in personal or group terms. On another 4 out of the 16 statements about half were unaware of any difference between the parties, and on the remaining 8, between one-third and nearly a half of the sample could detect no difference at all.[1]

There is now a great deal of similar evidence that seems to challenge the optimistic to formulate a theory of representative democracy capable of holding its own in face of the facts of political behaviour. If rational choice of any kind presupposes at least a modicum of relevant and accurate information, then it appears that the individual with the basic equipment for rational political participation is the exception rather than the rule. This perception has led some social scientists to account for the stability and change of political systems in ways that dispense with the notion of rationality at an individual level. Some have even argued that it is the indifference and ignorance of a large number of people towards the short-term benefits they could gain from active political participation that save our societies from being devoured by their inherent contradictions.[2] It might be more cautiously argued that countries like the United States or Great Britain have a surprising capacity to maintain the stability of their institutions, for a time at any rate, in the face of low levels of participation and widespread ignorance about the decisions that are actually being made in the name of the people. But

[1] These examples and many others are quoted by John C. Wahlke in 'Public Policy and Representative Government: the Role of the Represented', mimeographed paper presented to the International Political Science Association's World Congress, September 1967.

[2] T. Parsons, '"Voting" and the Equilibrium of the American Political System', in E. Burdick and A. Brodbeck (eds), *American Voting Behaviour*, (Free Press, 1959), and W. H. Morris-Jones, 'In Defence of Apathy', *Political Studies*, Vol. II, No. 1, 1954, pp. 25–37.

the evidence of impressive levels of straightforward ignorance and of elementary confusion about the alternatives offered by competing political organizations at least demands a reconsideration of the terms in which discussions about democracy and representation have been conducted. The message of the pollsters seems clear: the citizen of the modern democracies is not the figure he has been taken to be. Classical democratic theory, we are told, has tended to assume an individual capable of contributing from his own perspective to the process of discussion in a meaningful manner. The pollsters do find such individuals, but in alarmingly small numbers.[1]

A valid, if imperfectly reassuring, response to these anxieties is to point out that they set the dismal facts against a very simplistic notion of the arguments advanced at different times by the political theorists. What we have called traditional political theory is centrally concerned with advocacy, with ideal or at least preferable forms of political life, and facts that reveal the extent of the shortfall from an ideal cannot possibly invalidate it as a desirable state of affairs.[2] Furthermore, though arguments of disillusion are frequently advanced, it is often not clear what is being referred to as 'Classical Democratic Theory' in attacks on the naive assumptions behind earlier thought. Theorists have in the past elaborated models of representative systems on the basis of assumptions about the individual at least as pessimistic or 'realistic' as those that emerge inductively from the surveys. Indeed, the naiveté may be on the part of the social scientists. F. Marini has recently pointed out that we could have been spared some quite unnecessary expressions of dismay from social scientists who have misinterpreted, to the point of caricature, Locke's assumptions about citizens in a democracy.[3] Far from basing his model for a stable and successful polity on the discrete, rational citizen, Locke starts from a gloomy assessment of the individual, and takes it for granted that the individual cannot judge single acts, though he can, in the long run, judge whether the welfare of the citizen has been abused or not. This points towards a more complex definition of political choice and rationality than is always implicit in the survey studies, one that can take account not only of an aspect of what we refer to here as the process of Discussion, but also of the process of Security, the rule of law in the widest sense, and the processes of Power. The point here is not that Locke provided the comprehensive theory we are looking for, but that he recognized that anything as complex as a political system

---

[1] A. Campbell et al., The American Voter (Wiley, 1960), Ch. 9, 'Attitude Structure and the Problem of Ideology'.

[2] G. Duncan and S. Lukes, 'The New Democracy', Political Studies, Vol. XI, No. 2, June 1963, pp. 156–77.

[3] Frank Marini, 'John Locke and the Revision of Classical Democratic Theory', Western Political Quarterly, Vol. XXII, No. 1., March 1969, pp. 5–19.

cannot be reduced to simple dimensions. The system is not a macrocosm reflecting the processes of thought and choice of an idealized individual. On the contrary, a distinctive political system arises, in ways that are extraordinarily difficult to analyse and distinguish, from a combination of both the specific and the general predispositions of fallible individuals dispersed across complex social structures, mediated by a variety of institutions that have evolved unevenly over time.

The theorists, as Pitkin has argued particularly clearly in connection with the concept of representation, have explored different aspects of a most complex process with a subtlety that our improved resources for collecting some kinds of evidence must not encourage us to ignore.[1] We need a conceptual apparatus that begins to do justice to the complexity of the political interactions, one that will offset the natural tendency in rigorous empirical studies to suspect concepts that cannot be defined within the specific terms of the enquiry. Something as complex as political rationality cannot be explored only in terms of the limited criteria applied to the evidence cited above. Likewise the concept of Ideology may have been so narrowed in a distinguished American voting study as to mean little more than a particular kind of consistency.[2] The consistency among attitudes these authors so ingeniously measured may be an important aspect of the belief systems of mass publics, but it may not represent the only kind of coherence to be found there.

If many of the concepts we have inherited from earlier political theorists are ambiguous or inadequate, we have to continue a discussion that has not become simpler with time. Indeed, our ability to uncover fresh complications in new evidence, for example, about the nature of opinions and attitudes and the ways in which they can be modified, has yet to be matched by a corresponding fertility in the production of concepts and theories that will enable us to restate normative arguments about democracy and representation in fresh and compelling terms.

Individual opinions and sample surveys
Any bibliography of books directly or indirectly concerned with the study of public opinion will indicate the preponderance of American contributions to the field. James Bryce, Liberal MP for Aberdeen and British Ambassador to Washington between 1907 and 1913, observed in his classic study *The American Commonwealth* that, 'In no country is public opinion so powerful as in the United States: in no country can it be so well studied'.[3] What he chiefly had in mind was the strong Populist strain in the American politics of his time, but his judgment has been

---

[1] Pitkin, *The Concept of Representation* (University of California Press, 1967), Ch. 10.

[2] Campbell, loc. cit.

[3] James Bryce, *The American Commonwealth* (Macmillan, 1888), Ch. LXXVI.

confirmed for a number of other reasons, some to do with the generally strong development of the social sciences in American universities, and some, as we shall see, with the sheer availability of conveniently organized evidence. By contrast, British scholars have repeatedly lamented the tiresome incoherence, from their point of view, of the ways in which census and electoral data are collected in the United Kingdom.[1] For whatever reasons, Bryce's own shrewd commonsense account of the working of American public opinion has been superseded by increasingly sophisticated procedures, developed in several related fields, for generating evidence. Lecturing at Harvard in 1904, Bryce pointed out that much political theory had been too exclusively concerned with ethical and philosophical matters and that 'down even to the time of Hobbes and Locke, there was little attempt to base the ideas advanced upon actual observation of phenomena'. He went on to describe in general terms the social scientists' new method of observation, that of 'carefully examining phenomena, of recording them with the minutest particularity, of separating the relevant from the irrelevant—when we have arrived at the point where we can be sure that the matter discarded really is irrelevant—of critical analytical study of the materials obtained, of inference and generalization, and finally of the process of synthesis by which we endeavour to build up a system of generalization of observed and recorded fact'.[2] Developments in this direction, particularly since the Second World War, have been impressive, though in some ways, we have suggested, they have multiplied the problems of maintaining the links between what is actually observed and the ethical and philosophical considerations that should be directing the activity of observation.

Forty years after Bryce's Godkin lecture, a team of seven senior Harvard academics, including three clinical psychologists, three social psychologists and one social anthropologist, assisted by seventeen other investigators, conducted an intensive study, very much in the spirit of Bryce's remarks, into the opinions and personalities of ten men. To satisfy themselves that they had accumulated sufficient particular and relevant observations, they not only subjected their willing victims to the attentions of a large number of investigators, they also put them through twenty-seven different tests, designed to give information on distinct aspects of the individual's personality, attitudes and development, together with one long interview which explored the individuals' opinions with respect to a single, complex political object, Soviet Russia.[3] The object was to provide a set of observations of the psychological organiza-

[1] See D. Butler and D. Stokes, *Political Change in Britain* (Macmillan, 1969), p. 13, and Ch. 3 below.

[2] Quoted in E. S. A. Ions, *James Bryce* (Macmillan, 1968), p. 191.

[3] M. Brewster Smith, Jerome S. Bruner and Robert W. White, *Opinions and Personality* (Wiley, 1956).

tion of each individual, sufficiently complete to provide reliable inferences about the anchorage of a particular set of political opinions, their
degree of complexity and informational support, their importance to the
individual, the extent to which they serve as a vehicle to express much
more general hopes or anxieties, the extent to which they are absorbed
with little effort or attention from the individual's social environment.
Each subject was interviewed for thirty hours, and the final critical
analysis and synthesis took several years.

The authors claim that it should now be possible to repeat such
studies with substantially less effort and without significantly reducing
the pay-off, but even so this takes us a long way from the casual procedure of the polling organization's interviewer and even further from
the journalist who collects a few random opinions by buttonholing the
proverbial man in the street. A competent ecological study, that measures
the social distribution of opinions on, say, the Russian invasion of Czechoslovakia in 1968, is crude and ambiguous by comparison. Such a study
may find some degree of association between, for example, the youth of
those questioned and the intensity of their expressed reaction to that
event, and such a finding would suggest plausible inferences, but they
would have to remain highly tentative. This is so because, quite apart
from the technical problems involved in sampling large numbers of
opinions, the same verbal response to a structured question can represent
a substantial range of meanings in terms of what Newcomb, in his
definition of an attitude, sums up as the 'individual's organisation of
psychological processes'.[1] It is true that the authors of *Opinions and
Personality* can tell us little about the connections between the orientations they examine and the actual behaviour of their subjects, a state of
affairs that is very common in studies of attitudes and opinions, but they
do explore the specific area of opinion in great detail, and they can locate
the complex of opinion in a detailed context which specifies the organization of processes that so to speak hold the individual together psychologically: his level of information, general predisposition to seek or
avoid fresh information, the use made of information about the outside
world to establish a subjective sense of security or to play out unresolved
anxieties, the impact of his early experience, and his job expectations. It
is this psychological context that gives its full meaning to the opinion.
With it we can at least begin a discussion employing general theoretical
terms, such as rationality, because the observations provide us with
enough information to make qualitative distinctions between the
different patterns of emotion and knowledge that each individual set of
opinions reflects. Or, if we were interested in the political implications of
these opinions, their intensity, the extent to which they might be modi-

[1] T. M. Newcomb, 'On the Definition of Attitude', in M. Jahoda and N.
Warren, *Attitudes* (Penguin Modern Psychology, 1966).

fied by, or determine reactions to fresh information and new experiences, we would know enough, perhaps, to make reasonable projections from such a detailed dissection.

But the problems are obvious and suggest a variant of V. O. Key's dry observation that public opinion is 'those opinions of private persons which governments find it prudent to heed'.[1] We could add that public opinion is whatever survives the crude limitations of our resources for identifying and describing it. Clearly we cannot generalize about public opinion on the basis of ten individual case studies, and, equally clearly, once we start working with the kind of numbers that sampling theory requires for the reduction of the possible margin of error to acceptable proportions, we cannot possibly hope to study any single individual in such depth. Not only will we be likely, within the kind of resources normally available for such projects, to secure the attention of each individual for a shorter period of time, but we will also have to sacrifice much of the contextual material in order to find room for a wider range of opinions and attitudes on specifically political issues. For example, the recent study by Butler and Stokes, *Political Change in Britain*, is based on a sample of about 2,000 people, each of whom was interviewed three times, on each occasion for approximately one hour. Each individual who was successfully interviewed on all three occasions provided more than 1,200 distinct items of information, from age, sex and occupation, to opinions about current issues and complex beliefs of the kind many people find it hard to formulate, about the nature of social class and parties in Britain.[2] The business of processing such a quantity of data, from a sample that is representative of the whole population, in an attempt to distinguish the relevant determinants of attitudes and of behaviour from all the possible long-run and short-run forces playing more or less unevenly through an entire society, is demanding indeed. Whatever its success, it cannot aim at the refinement and complexity of a clinical analysis. There will be a more or less substantial loss of information. But it should be clear that, to the extent that we cannot place particular political attitudes and opinions into some kind of context, we defocus our observation of actual phenomena and confuse the issues raised in any more general theoretical analysis of mass participation in the process of Discussion.

This stress on the complexity of the phenomena and the crudity and limitations of our resources for observing them is very necessary. We do not have a science here that is predictive or even precisely descriptive. We cannot, after all, directly observe the psychological processes (complex and often obscure) which we label as attitudes or opinions. We must make inferences from collections of verbal responses and, where we are dealing with the more distant past, even more indirectly from voting behaviour itself. The best we can expect are approximations and statements about major characteristics and general tendencies. We will do well if we can combine some of the advantages of the intensive study that concentrates on a psychological level of analysis, with the opportunities provided by the large-scale survey for charting the broad currents and cross-currents that affect the general public. This kind of evidence can then become part of an historical analysis of what Bryce referred to as the curious process of the 'mutual action and reaction of the makers or leaders of opinion upon the mass, and of the mass upon them'.[1]

Psychological and sociological analysis
Our requirements suggest a simple analytical framework for organizing a systematic investigation of the role of the general public. Specific studies will fill out different parts of the framework, but no single aspect can stand on its own. The problem for any broader theoretical and philosophical analysis is to try and relate the different dimensions of the framework one to another, to examine, without getting bogged down in undirected empiricism, 'the duality and tension between purpose and institutionalization' to which Pitkin refers. So, for convenience sake, we can begin by making a few straightforward analytical distinctions, in the understanding that they *are* analytical distinctions and that the dimensions of actual behaviour that we seek to shred out are always inextricably interwoven in the actual social processes we need to understand.

Opinions and Personality is quite exclusively concerned with one dimension of the analytical framework, the *psychological level of analysis*, that is to say, with the determinants and interconnections of the subjective processes within the individual. There are occasions when narrowly focused and intensive analysis at this level is of great interest to the student of politics.[2] But when it comes to looking at the general public, or at least at large samples taken from the general public, we need to simplify matters in ways that might grate on the sophisticated sensibilities of the clinical psychologist. We need to be able to discriminate between different orders of psychological organization, but in terms that are manageable within the limitations of survey analysis. We shall distinguish between three layers, as it were, under the general headings of Personality, Attitude and Opinion.[3] Personality refers to those aspects

---

[1] James Bryce, op. cit., Ch. LXXVI.

[2] See, e.g., A. L. George and J. L. George, *Woodrow Wilson and Colonel House*, New York, 1956.

[3] These distinctions are used by H. McClosky in 'Psychological Correlates of Foreign Policy Attitudes', in Rosenau (ed.), *Domestic Sources of Foreign Policy* (Free Press, 1967), and reprinted in H. McClosky, *Political Inquiry* (Collier-

of an individual's orientation to life that are acquired early and deeply ingrained, a relatively stable compound of genetic endowment and early learning and socialization. Psychologists have devoted much theoretical and practical ingenuity to the problems of identifying and assessing these basic orientations to life, and it is fair to say that the field of Personality Theory is far from being coherent or harmonious, but we can afford to be eclectic with respect to competing theories of personality.[1] Though we must always be tentative about the existence of any hypothetical personality dimension, the characteristics that psychologists provisionally distinguish from each other do tend to go together in clusters or groups, forming more general personality predispositions. So, though we cannot directly observe an attitude or an opinion, it is possible to devise questionnaire scales, which catch echoes from different components of a general psychological syndrome. A questionnaire scale, very roughly, combines questions inviting reactions to a particular object or concept, which will enable respondents with similar reactions to be grouped together and compared with other groups located at different points along the same stretch of 'psychological space'.[2] If these scales function consistently and interrelate in theoretically plausible ways, we can combine them into measures of general personality predispositions which could turn out to be significant determinants of political attitudes, opinion and behaviour. For instance, a construct that emerges as important in McClosky's studies is the inflexible or aversive personality predisposition, which is reflected in the measurements of a large number of carefully prepared and tested scales, each of them designed to tap a distinguishable component of the syndrome. These scales include measures of intolerance of ambiguity, guilt, dominance, ethnocentrism, alienation, anomy,[3] and two measures of dichotomous thinking. Individuals who appear on what these researchers like to refer to with macabre familiarity as the 'sick end' of any one of these scales, tend also to appear towards the 'sick end' of the others. Since these questionnaires can conveniently be administered to large samples, it becomes possible to distinguish in an approximate way between categories of respondent that evince the aversive personality syndrome in different degrees. One can then proceed to compare these categories in terms of their other characteristics, their attitudes, their opinions, their

---

Macmillan, 1969). The latter volume also contains a brief but comprehensive discussion of the possibilities offered by survey techniques, and their limitations.

[1] C. Hall and G. Lindzey, *Theories of Personality* (Wiley, 1957).

[2] F. Kerlinger, *Foundations of Behavioural Research* (Holt, Rinehart & Winston, 1964), Ch. 27.

[3] The reasons for this spelling of anomy are given in McClosky and Schaar, 'Four Dimensions of Anomy', *American Sociological Review*, Vol. 30, No. 1, Feb. 1965, pp. 14–40. Reprinted in H. McClosky, *Political Inquiry*.

class, level of education, race, or anything else for which we have descriptive data. We might then, and this of course is the object of this kind of analysis, be able not only to provide a more intricate description of our population, but also to make inferences about cause and effect. Some of these are chicken and egg problems and can never finally be resolved, but some are, as we shall see, open to systematic analysis.

However, this anticipates a later discussion. The main point here is that it is possible to take soundings, even in large samples, of the broad distribution of deeply rooted and stable psychological characteristics, which comprise what McClosky refers to as Personality. Obviously, the more frequent the soundings and the more various the instruments that are used, the more confidence we can have in our inferences. But it is none the less possible to pick up *something* from this level with much cruder instrumentation. The Berkeley project uses a great many measures. But one analysis of American opinion poll data on the Viet-Nam war, for example, distinguished two groups of respondents, 'worriers' and 'nonworriers'. On the basis of decidedly limited questionnaire data it seemed possible to infer a general disposition to worry that was unrelated to party or any identifiable group membership.[1] There was a slight tendency on the part of 'worriers' to favour de-escalation of the war. But with such a simple measure the finding is merely suggestive and can hardly be said to establish a link between an underlying personality disposition and a specific issue orientation.

The second level we refer to is that of Attitudes. Here we are concerned still with relatively stable predispositions and beliefs, but these are less part of the basic psychological structure of the individual, and are therefore to some degree vulnerable to the impact of fresh experience. They are more specifically attached to various stimuli, for example communists, black men, the Tory party or students; they are difficult to dislodge partly because they may actually be indirect expressions of underlying personality traits, and partly because they will be part of the cognitive and affective structure through which the individual identifies himself with the social groups that sustain him and help him develop a sense of personal identity. Examples of Attitude scales from McClosky include measures of pro-business attitudes, classical conservatism, economic conservatism, left wing sympathies, fascist sympathies. There is no clear line to be drawn between personality and attitude. For instance, it would be hard to place the celebrated and much-disputed F-scale in Adorno's *Authoritarian Personality*.[2] But there is clearly a distinction to be made. For example, attitudes strongly fostered by the individual's reference groups may conflict with his underlying dispo-

---

[1] S. Verba *et al.*, 'Public Opinion and the War in Viet Nam', *The American Political Science Review*, Vol. LXI, No. 2, June 1967, pp. 317–33.

[2] T. W. Adorno *et. al.*, *The Authoritarian Personality* (Harper & Row, 1950).

sition.[1] His 'conversion' might be correspondingly swift or extreme if he were suddenly to find himself in a very different social environment, or with a new and different set of opportunities for political expression and activity.

Finally, there is the level of Opinions on issues, the level at which the newspaper opinion poll is normally operating. The stimulus here will be something more specific and time-bound, a politician, a decision, a proposal, a policy.

Opinions we think of as articulated responses and judgments. We may, of course, infer the existence of more general and rooted attitudes from statements of opinion, if we have enough statements that relate to each other in theoretically plausible ways. A consistent set of responses to questions on public policy towards coloured immigrants, referring to housing, education, jobs, social behaviour, religious practices, and so on, may indicate a general attitude of hostility or acceptance. But the individual responses may merely reflect the respondent's notion of what the interviewer wants to hear, or a judgment picked up from others pretty much at random and without any investment of thought or emotional energy. Or again, the responses may reflect a strongly-felt judgment on a specific situation which is closely related to more general orientations, and stimulated by salient political events. We need to be able to distinguish the more time-bound and specific level of opinions because any political development may mobilize a great variety of less articulate predispositions and transient anxieties under the same programmatic and opinionative banner.[2]

At this point we must introduce the second dimension of our analytical framework, the *sociological level of analysis*. It is of course a truism to say that it is virtually impossible to make any significant statements about individual behaviour and belief without referring directly or indirectly to the individual's relationships with others. Even our most distinctive and personal characteristics are developed though interaction with others. However, the influence of the social environment or environments through which we move will vary widely over time, both with respect to the patterns of influences that are brought to bear on the individual, and the salience or the intensity with which they are perceived. From the moment we first draw breath we are subject to constant invasions by our social environment, at one time leading to effective assimilation, at another to a more temporary colonization. In what we refer to here as

---

[1] See the suggestive illustration of this point in a discussion of a field experiment concerned with the introduction of innovations into the farming practices of two contrasted communities in M. Rokeach, 'Attitude Change and Behavioural Change', *Public Opinion Quarterly*, Vol. XXX, No. 4, Winter 1966, pp. 529–51.

[2] See F. Parkin, *Middle Class Radicalism* (Manchester University Press, 1968), Chs. 4, 5 and 6, and the discussion in Ch. 5, below.

Personality, but also in our Attitudes, we are all the victims or beneficiaries of our early formative relationships and experiences. The people we look to, whether with satisfaction or with mistrust, are constantly feeding us with cues through which to interpret the social reality that confronts us, as well as with threats and inducements to adjust our behaviour and beliefs.

In order to relate the psychological level of analysis to this sociological context, we can place the distinctions borrowed from McClosky alongside a set of distinctions that are congruent, if not precisely parallel to them. These have been suggested by Herbert Kelman as a setting for the analysis of social influence.[1] Kelman roughly distinguishes three processes of social influence, which he calls Compliance, Identification and Internalization. There is a rough, but only rough, correspondence between this simple hierarchy and the one borrowed from McClosky. Taken together, they provide a setting within which we may consider the complex interplay that we have placed under the broad democratic norm of Discussion. 'Compliance can be said to occur when an individual accepts influence from another person or from a group because he hopes to achieve a favourable reaction from the other. . . . He does not adopt the induced behaviour—for example, a particular opinion response— because he believes in its content, but because it is instrumental in the production of a satisfying social effect.' 'Identification can be said to occur when an individual adopts behaviour derived from another person or group because this behaviour is associated with a satisfying self-defining relationship to this person or group.' Examples of this would be the normal and perhaps essential imitation of parental attitudes and actions by children, or in the more or less conscious process of learning to conform to the standards required of a new occupational role. 'Internalization can be said to occur when an individual accepts influence because the induced behaviour is congruent with his value system.'

We are not suggesting, of course, a simple correspondence between, say, the process of Compliance and the psychology of Opinions. The balance between the two schemes is uneven. One might believe entirely in the rightness of an opinion that one learns in a group with which one strongly identifies, or that fits clearly with one's general value system. However, most of us, if we are frankly introspective, have to recognize that many of our opinions are disguised bids for approval or acceptance. On the other hand, what we have been discussing as attitudes are not the product of Compliance, though many of them are strongly internalized.

But some of the implications of this link between the psychological and the sociological levels of analysis should be clear. We are concerned, in analysing the role of the General Public, with groups of people, by

[1] H. C. Kelman, 'Three Processes of Social Influence', in M. Jahoda and N. Warren (eds), *Attitudes*, op. cit., p. 151.

no means mutually exclusive and often in flux. Politics consists of the disagreements and agreements of these groups as these are perceived and engineered by individuals through some form of collective action. The interpretation placed on these perceptions, their salience for different groups, the degree and nature of the interconnections between different levels of predisposition and the 'social reality' of the group, all these factors are determinants of or constraints on political outcomes, limiting or creating options for political decision-makers or others who wish to produce or forestall change. If we can devise means to place a not too simplistic descriptive account of the different broad types of predisposition into its social context, by identifying the perceptions individuals have of their relationships to groups or categories of people with whom they do or do not identify themselves and by whom they are positively or negatively influenced, we will have some insight into the empirical reality to which our questions about representation, rationality, and opposition refer. Surveys are only one kind of evidence we can use for this purpose, but since they are the best available means of getting approximately accurate inside knowledge of the value systems and perceptions of large numbers of people, it is worth at this point considering the opportunities they provide for systematic analysis, as opposed to mere description.

This kind of analysis depends on the collection of two kinds of evidence, firstly, detailed evidence of what it is we want to explain (attitudes, opinions, forms of behaviour), and secondly as much evidence as possible on all the possible significant determinants of that behaviour (broadly speaking, all the characteristics of the individual that will indirectly reflect the formative experiences he has been through, his age, occupation, sex, occupational and other group memberships and identifications, and so on). It is important to stress that these data are indices, indirect clues to complex social processes. If we find a strong association, for instance, between socio-economic class and party identification, we may say that class largely determines voting behaviour, but this is the crudest shorthand for a rich interplay of conditions and circumstances. Neither must we overlook that, as in all sociological explanation, some data will find its place in both collections; in the processes of social interaction the outcome of one set of factors will be one of the determinants of another, and we must consider it both as dependent and as independent variable.

Collecting some of the evidence is a very straightforward business; most people are clearly either male or female, for instance. But group membership may be harder to define; it is likely to be more useful to define a union member as someone who identifies with his union in addition to performing the minimal gesture of paying his dues, and in that case we will need a measure of the extent or *degree* to which he identifies. Opinions may raise further problems; two people may express the same degree of disapproval of the Russian invasion of Czechoslovakia, but one of them may not know that the victim is a supposedly communist country and this degree of ignorance might affect our assessment of the significance of the opinion. When we move on to Attitudes or Personality, as we have seen, the problems are greater still, since the dimensions of both are more obscure and problematic. However, if the questions have been aptly formulated, we can reduce the responses into quantitative terms that express the approximate *relative* positions of different groups and categories of people with respect to such dimensions as, say, social deference, tolerance of racial minorities, support for entry into the Common Market, or whatever concerns us from the various layers of our psychological dimension. Because we have data on the social and behavioural characteristics of the respondents, their occupations, political participation, and so on, we can, as it were, plot these various group averages on to the different parts of the social structure, which will be useful for further analysis under our general rubric of Power. Because, if we use the appropriate statistics, we can interrelate the means that reflect the relative distribution of personality type, attitude, opinion, level of information, we can arrive at a rough chart indicating the level (both in a quantitative and a qualitative sense) of what we are calling Discussion.[1] A descriptive analysis will tell us what goes with what, and, depending on the success of our various measures of degree, to what extent, in approximate and relative terms.

However, a more explanatory kind of analysis raises other problems. A description may hint at the workings of processes of social influence. But we need to be able to manipulate our evidence further if we are to account for what we can describe. For example, there is the familiar correlation between trade-union membership and support of the Labour Party, which is high, as is hardly surprising. But Butler and Stokes point out:[2] 'As is so often the case in social analysis, the key to interpreting the correlation of union membership and party support lies in reaching a reasonable view of their temporal or causal sequence.' In the light of evidence their survey collected about the reasons for joining unions, they produce a case for reversing what is generally assumed to be the direction of the causal sequence. Contrary to a common assumption, it is more frequently true that party support leads to union membership than the other way round, an inversion that 'puts a very different face on the observed political cleavage between members and non-members'.

We will look at other examples of explanatory problems, for instance

[1] For technical discussions, see Kerlinger, op. cit., and W. Torgerson, *Theory and Methods of Scaling* (Wiley, 1968).

[2] Butler and Stokes, op. cit., p. 157.

the reasons for working-class conservative voting. The point here is that the systematic analysis of survey data can make substantial contributions to causal explanation. It can never provide definitive answers; even where there are consistent and strong associations between an antecedent and a consequent factor, we can never *prove* that the association is not determined by some third factor of which we are unaware and, as we have pointed out before, we can only discriminate roughly between the influence of one factor—for instance some degree of class consciousness—and another with which it is inextricably involved—for instance the aquisition of a sense of party identification through imitation of one's parents well before the implications of political choice are realized.[1] However, this kind of analysis will have done a great deal if it does no more than dispose of commonly accepted assumptions, such as the one on trade-union membership just referred to. The pursuit of causal explanation through the systematic analysis sketchily described here helps to place the complex distribution of characteristics caught in the cross-sections of the surveys into the context of a process of change over time, the context that the more professional political actors respond to in the curious process of their interaction with the stirrings of a General Public.

Rationality, social reality, and history
The broad framework suggested here for the psychological and sociological levels of analysis carries no implications for the potential *political* importance of any of the dimensions we have distinguished. From the point of view of a clinical psychologist, the deeply rooted and underlying predispositions of the individual may be more interesting and significant, whilst opinions may be too variable or too limited to specific situations to reflect the subjective processes in which he is interested. However, political history is replete with instances of occasions when a transitory shift of opinion, running through strategically located groups at the right time, has had consequences of great importance. Such shifts of mood or 'sentiment', to use Bryce's term, may or may not be based on inaccurate information or lead to socially damaging repercussions. Where they tend to, we hope to be able to look to the protection and incentives provided by our institutional arrangements to encourage judgement in the light of superior information, experience and foresight. The institutionalization of representative roles may serve to muffle irrational pressures.

However, the issue of rationality cannot be so simply disposed of at this level. We cannot safely identify the process of rationality with

---

[1] D. Easton and R. Hess, 'The Child's Political World', *Midwest Journal of Political Science*, Vol. 6, August 1962, pp. 229–46.

coherently justified judgments, based on a high level of accurate information. Objective, realistic perceptions are by definition a desirable and must be a necessary condition of a rational process of any kind, but it would be wrong to refer to them as a sufficient condition, because the notion of objective reality is in social and political relations a highly ambiguous one. The problem here is a particularly important example of the way in which inductive inquiry by social scientists seems to complicate the terms of our more general philosophical argument.

One of the ten subjects of the investigation described in *Opinions and Personality*, given the name of John Chatwell, emerges as particularly well informed and aware. Asked to describe what sort of person he would most like to be, he responds:

'I like to see a man stick his neck out. And I like to see a man who has figured out the angles, too. I always enjoy meeting a man who has really thought a problem out and hasn't overlooked anything. I generally feel a little contemptuous of a fellow who makes a pronouncement or adopts a course of action or something of that sort, where there is some fairly obvious factor in the situation that he has either overlooked or discounted that destroys the validity of the position or course he has adopted'.

The authors point out that this remark illustrates two of Chatwell's basic motivations. Keen argument satisfied a decided relish for aggressive competition, but his need for understanding was also vital to him 'as a generalized means of mastering the unknown by rationality'.[1] Clearly, for Chatwell, this process involved getting on top of a good deal of factual information. Equally it involved developing a highly integrated and internally consistent set of beliefs and opinions. More than for most people, there seems to have been a self-conscious coherence and articulation to his orientation towards the outside world, including such remote facts of life as Soviet Russia, which strike one immediately as being characteristic of an impressively rational individual. However, as Kelman points out, we need to distinguish between the internal coherence of a belief system, which has been perfectly internalized by an individual, and its rationality. This is so because the facts on which social judgments are based are not facts in the sense in which we use the word to apply to natural phenomena. Objective facts in that sense may be relevant to social judgments, but what creates problems for the notion of rationality is the existence of 'social facts', or a 'social reality' which is embedded in the unanalysed assumptions about the nature of existence that are sustained by a particular social context, and which come, as Berger and Luckman have argued, to be seen as facts in a special sense.

[1] Smith *et. al.*, op. cit., p. 100.

We come to reify what is man-made and essentially temporary, and thus merge our world of institutions into the world of what is really 'out there' in the world of nature.[1] The contingent forms of a society, which have been evolved over time, its structure of social relations, its institutions and the shared values that give them their legitimacy, become reified and regarded as right because they are there. The subjective identity of the individual is a precarious thing and depends on his relationships with other individuals who are significant to him, and this can only occur through a language of common assumptions about the nature of social life. These assumptions can be coherent and effective in maintaining its stabilities of institution and attitude, but we may on other grounds find them irrational. Kelman points out that he would still 'characterize as internalization the adoption of beliefs because of their congruence with a value system that is basically *irrational*. Thus an authoritarian individual may adopt certain racist attitudes because they fit into his paranoid, irrational view of the world. . . . Similarly, it should be noted that congruence with a person's value system does not necessarily imply logical consistency. Behaviour would be congruent, if in some way or other it fitted into the person's value system, if it seemed to belong there and be demanded by it'.[2]

In other words, rationality is not a matter of the mythical ideal individual democrat, evaluating 'facts' and contributing his judgment and voice to what is in principle an objective process of discussion. We can look at aspects of rationality at the individual level, but the argument centres on the nature of the society that has come out of history, the product of contingent political decisions and not of impersonal laws of development, the values maintained by its institutions, the nature of the legitimacy they have acquired, the possibilities they tend to foreclose. What we need here are judgments about values, not logical or scientific proofs. It is of course one of the functions of political opposition in democratic political systems to keep open the questions revolving round these values, and the function of Security to make that function a genuine possibility.

The distinction being made here is well illustrated by considering the phenomenon sometimes referred to as 'brain-washing'. The purpose of the kind of 'thought reform' described by Robert Lifton[3] is less to create confusion about objective facts, than to produce a coherent, highly internalized and positively valued social reality, first of all by depriving the individual of his sense of subjective identity by isolating him from

---

[1] P. Berger and T. Luckman, *The Social Construction of Reality* (Doubleday, 1966).
[2] loc. cit., p. 156.
[3] Robert J. Lifton, *Thought Reform and the Psychology of Totalism* (Norton, 1961).

his social contacts, and then allowing him to recover it, but under carefully controlled conditions that induce him through fear and loneliness to comply with—hopefully to internalize—the consistent and unchallengeable orientations of his new companions. The programme of the thought reformers is based on sound social psychology: it merely seeks to refine and concentrate the normal processes of social interaction in one direction and for one purpose. The nature of these general processes have most important implications for any analysis of the role of the General Public in the process of representation in democracies. In many areas, more important than ignorance of factual information or of the details of particular issues are more general orientations towards different institutions or political activities. Habit and a generalized sense of convenience and security, as well as the distribution of the various forms of social power, one of which is a general sense of the legitimacy of the existing state of affairs, contribute considerably to the powers of survival of political and social institutions. There is an historical legacy in the process of institutionalization, which may promote stability but will also inhibit and mould responses to a rapidly changing environment and changing possibilities. What V. O. Key has aptly described as the 'viscous' process of change in mass publics is partly a function of the intrinsic inertia of institutional arrangements, partly of the place they come to fill and the values associated with them in the eyes of the public. Necessarily the third dimension of the analytical framework we are suggesting is an *historical level of analysis*.

Students of politics have a great deal to gain from insights into the nature of social/psychological man in the work of scholars in other fields. However, as the social psychologist Henri Tajfel has pointed out, these levels of analysis 'cannot provide an explanation of large-scale historical or social events. Each case of co-operation or of conflict must be understood in its own right, in terms of its own conditions, and determinants, which may be economic or social, political or historical, and are most often a mixture of all these'.[1] We may interpret these events in the light of what we learn about the way in which different types of individual adapt to and act on their social environments, but these social environments are the product of contingent decisions by men in the past, choices that could have been made otherwise, discoveries and random occurrences. Any serious and systematic analysis of public opinion and attitudes must be sensitive to this historical context. Thus, the 1962 survey, which provides fresh evidence for an analysis of the political significance of social class in Runciman's *Relative Deprivation and Social Justice*, is preceded by a long discussion of the historical background that dwells on the major events of war, educational changes and economic change,

[1] Henri Tajfel, 'Co-operation between Human Groups', *The Eugenics Review*, Vol. 58, No. 2, June 1966, pp. 77–84.

that have altered in complex ways the patterns of co-operation and conflict among groups and have in consequence led to shifts in the aspirations and perceptions of the individuals who identify with them.[1] Butler and Stokes have incorporated an aspect of the historical dimension into their survey by dividing their sample into four 'political generations'; consisting of those who went through their most impressionable years of adolescence or early adulthood in each of four broadly distinguishable periods: pre-1918, interwar, post-1945, and post-1951.[2] Social and political relationships and the anxieties, tensions and possibilities these entailed for different groups, changed very substantially in many respects over this period of time. It seems reasonable to assume that the experience of going through the Depression years, for example, would develop deeply-rooted attitudes and perceptions that would have quite distinctive properties for many groups. The traditional solidarity of the mining community owes much to the fierce economic and political pressures of the 1920s, and attitudes engendered then have been preserved by the community's insulation from other groups. Distinctive attitudes towards the political parties, and more general attitudes towards the legitimacy of the actual distribution of power in British society would have become part of the social reality of that political generation and, depending on the intensity of the formative experience, these well-established predispositions would in turn be used to interpret and mould responses to subsequent events and experiences.

Again, we must avoid suggesting that these historical pressures were in any simple sense impersonal or inevitable, though that was how many regarded them at the time.[3] Bryce's curious process of interaction between political elites and political publics leaves some latitude of response open to the elites themselves, and how they react to their own problems of survival and the acquisition of power will affect not only opinions on the passing issues of the day, but may reinforce or modify broader, relatively stable and internalized attitudes towards the structure of the system, and the distribution of power. The appeal of Conservatism to the working class, for example, which cannot be explained on the basis of any *a priori* psychological process, has carefully cherished historical foundations. In their study of working-class Conservatives in urban England, McKenzie and Silver have analysed the flood of popular party literature that has stressed a few basic themes with relentless consistency since 1897. 'The central argument which emerges in the popular party literature is that the Conservatives are uniquely qualified to govern Britain and that the institutions of the country are safe in their

---

[1] G. Runciman, *Relative Deprivation and Social Justice* (University of California, 1962).
[2] op. cit., Ch. 3.
[3] Runciman, op. cit., p. 60.

hands alone.'[1] Party propaganda has dwelt on the malice and incompetence of the opposition, and has identified the Conservative Party with the national institutions, the monarchy, the House of Lords, and the established economic order, and with a national as opposed to a sectional interest, which was expressed in terms of a well-publicized concern for the working man. Within six years of its establishment in 1867, the Head Office of the National Union had distributed 'some eight hundred thousand pamphlets and circulars (four-fifths of them without charge), a very considerable figure when it is kept in mind that the newly enfranchised electorate after 1867 represented a total of approximately one million'. These were aimed directly at the new electors, with such titles as *Conservative Legislation for the Working Classes* and *The Political Future of the Working Classes, or Who are the Real Friends of the People*?[2] This kind of appeal exploited and helped to maintain attitudes of mutual obligation, deference and consensus, among different strata and groups, which had of course matured in English society for centuries before the electoral reforms of the 1860s. Certainly they were not an exclusively Tory inheritance.[3]

In a subtle analysis of the complex stirrings and infusions of groups that went to make up the Liberal Party of the nineteenth century, John Vincent has suggested that 'Perhaps 250 M.P.s altogether constituted the plain of the English (Liberal) Party, homogeneous in its pubic school and university education, its social advantages, and its Anglicanism, and this preponderance of numbers made its mark on the party character. It prevented it from being a revolutionary, a democratic, a crusading or doctrinal party: but gave to the party that spirit of equity and disinterestedness, uninflamed by ardour, that was its real merit in the 1860s. . . . Given the conditions of mid-Victorian England—a country equally divided between agriculture and industry, with its national education sharply cut off from the life of the great towns—the mass of easy-going landowners, lawyers and gentlemen of leisure who made up the inert majority of Parliamentary Liberals were better fitted to be the instruments of justice towards, at least, the urban populations, than any other section of the rich. What, in terms of an electoral system, was an anomalous, and unjust predominance of property in general, and certain kind of property, education, creed, and profession in particular, worked for the best in terms of the total national life'.[4] In both parties, the style of the representative process, the nature of the relationship between

[1] R. McKenzie and A. Silver, *Angels in Marble: Working Class Conservatives in Urban England* (Heineman, 1968). p. 72.

[2] Ibid., p. 43, and see also McKenzie, *British Political Parties* (Heineman, second edition 1964), pp. 159 ff.

[3] S. Beer, *Modern British Politics* (Faber, 1965), Ch. III.

[4] John Vincent, *The Formation of the Liberal Party* (Constable, 1966), p. 27.

political leaders and their followers, was implicit in a well-diffused acceptance of the existing hierarchical distribution of political functions and privileges between different groups and strata of society. It has been the achievement of the Conservative Party, assisted by the defection of Joseph Chamberlain to the Conservatives in 1886, with his working-class following in the Midlands, by the fragmentation of the Liberal Party leadership after the First World War, and by the relatively cautious challenge of the Labour Party thereafter, to succeed in identifying itself as an organization with the commanding features of this national consensus.[1] Recent surveys show repeatedly the evidence of the durability of such general attitudes, and of the tensions they can produce in individuals for whom they embody self-evident facts of life that seem at the same time to conflict with their equally self-evident economic interest. They are associated with the group identifications and polarizations that anchor the individual in his own social reality, helping to structure his perceptions in ways that may at times seem to be at odds with a simplistic notion of rationality as the pursuit of economic self-interest, but serving important purposes for the quality of his day-to-day relationships within his family or at work, and satisfying other, non-economic, priorities. The shape that the past imposes on the present, whether it is maintained by unreflecting habits and undisturbed assumptions, skilfully exploited by existing elites, or by constraints which individuals would challenge if they felt that they had the power to do so, is the complex premise within which we must pursue our investigation of the nature of socio/ psychological man. But our concern cannot be simply with description, however, complex. The problem for contemporary political analysis is the difficult one of attempting to order a description of the political process that may be growing increasingly complex, or merely increasingly fragmentary and confusing, in terms of ideas that identify the major objectives and functions of political activity. Our immediate purpose here is to use our broad analytical perspectives to throw some light on different aspects of the process of political representation.

[1] Trevor Wilson, *The Downfall of the Liberal Party*, 1914–1935 (Collins, 1966); and see in particular, Ralph Miliband, *Parliamentary Socialism* (Allen & Unwin, 1961).

3

Leaders and Voters

Perspectives of leaders and activists

'Bringing men up to the polls', wrote Bryce, 'is like passing a steam-roller over stones newly laid on the road: the angularities are pressed down, and an appearance of smooth and even uniformity is given which did not exist before. When a man has voted, he is committed; he has thereafter an interest in backing the view which he has sought to make prevail'.[1] The steamroller effect is partly a consequence of the crude and obvious institutional fact that in the British party system the diversity of political pressures and perceptions are channelled through only two main parties, but it is also a consequence of a subtler process of group identification and acquiescence, a psychological investment in a broad political orientation which is certain not to express the priorities of the individual at every point. The bi-polar structure of our party system, established in remote conflicts between King and Parliament and in the later formation of coalitions among generations of parliamentary elites, has, at both levels, the effect of a magnetic field that organises new issues as they emerge.[2] Since the rules and norms of partisan competition are solidly established in our institutional arrangements and since the pay-off for success, undivided control of the national government, is certain, there is an incentive for party elites to pursue the strategy of assembling a set of issue positions that can be presented as a challenging alternative to what is offered by the opposition. This process is certain to entail a degree of opportunism; however, politicians are not competing for support in an idealized open market—though the analogy has a considerable theoretical interest—and the party's general orientations are bound to reflect the perspectives and interests of the possibly quite disparate groups from which its leaders emerge and the compound of

[1] Bryce, *The American Commonwealth* (Macmillan, 1888), p. 5.
[2] There is a general discussion in P. Pulzer, *Political Representation and Elections in Britain* (Allen & Unwin, 1967); Ch. 2, 'Parties and the Electoral System.' See also J. H. Plumb, *The Growth of Political Stability in England, 1672–1725* (Macmillan, 1967).

specific issues that are salient to them.[1] The Liberal Party, to the distinctive Scottish wing of which Bryce belonged, developed as a highly heterogenous mass party after the electoral reforms of the 1860s. In addition to the landowners, lawyers and gentlemen of leisure who made up the 'inert majority' of the parliamentary party, there were the Liberal peerage, the radical dissenting businessmen of Yorkshire and Lancashire, together with their working-class support in the mining districts and Cromwellian counties, and others whose manifest opportunism threatened the kind of style that Gladstone, in particular, was trying to create for the party.[2] The strategy demanded by the need to secure a base of support in the new mass electorate strongly encouraged the development of effective national organization, and the development of a unifying Liberal perspective. To different degrees at different levels of political involvement, Liberalism became a shared general perspective that served to conceal from at least some of its adherents the unobserved angularities that remained. As Bryce hints, the formation of major coalitions is not merely a mechanical consequence of the options permitted by the structure of existing institutions; it may at some levels involve a degree of self-deception and irrationality. Vincent shows, for example, the extent to which Gladstone came to represent liberalism for a substantial proportion of his mass following, which identified him very strongly with the aspirations of its own reference groups, but on the basis of slender and ambiguous evidence from his own statements and behaviour. 'Gladstone practised no deception, but many were grossly deceived, when they assumed that Gladstone's own conscientiousness implied agreement with their own notions.'[3]

Furthermore, the self-deception is by no means only on the side of the party followers. Party leaderships never have full and accurate information on all their supporters and potential supporters. Like any other group, they have a normal capacity for seeing what they want to see. The implications of this aspect of the interaction between party leaders and party followers have not always been recognized either by academics or by politicians. In a phrase that has been used of political parties on both sides of the Atlantic, a process of 'gentle reification' has taken place that has had paradoxical effects,[4] on the one hand exaggerating the ideological and organizational coherence of the parties and on the other

[1] See A. Downs, *An Economic Theory of Democracy* (Harper & Row, 1957); but also a critique by D. Stokes, 'Spatial Models of Party Competition', *The American Political Science Review*, LVII, June 1963.

[2] J. Vincent, op. cit.

[3] Vincent, ibid., p. 234.

[4] D. Butler and D. Stokes, *Political Change in Britain* (Macmillan, 1969), p. 23; and D. Stokes, 'Parties and the Rationalisation of Electoral Forces' in Walter Dean Burnham (ed.), *American Party Systems* (Oxford University Press, 1967), p. 182.

hand, by endowing the parties with qualities of permanence and reality, affecting people's perceptions of the political universe, the interests that are being effectively represented and the possibilities that are available.

This tendency to invest the parties with a kind of reality they have seldom possessed appears in the arguments about party organization that have continued, from the days of the National Union and the National Liberal Federation of the late 1860s and early 1870s, up to the present. Party organization down to the grass roots has been seen by the leadership as an essential means of maintaining a mass following and impressing upon it the general and particular perspectives of the party. A substantial share of the blame for electoral defeat is invariably attributed to the cyclical delapidation of party machinery.

However, without denying the importance of grass-roots organization in modern mass parties, the activity of running the constituency parties is likely to spread the party orthodoxy round the local activists and party workers, who of course represent a very small proportion of the electorate, but is very much less likely to reach down into the bulk of the electorate. Even in the period when the careers of Randolph Churchill and Joseph Chamberlain seemed to give particular importance to the national party organizations, the juggernaut of party machinery barely kept pace with an expanding electorate. The broad bases of the party coalitions were pressed roughly into shape by other means, through the identification of local elites with different national leaders, and through the clear indications provided by the new popular press of the alignments of major groups in society, for example the alignment of the Labour 'aristocracy' and religious dissent with Liberalism. The related claim for mass party organization, that it serves to channel opinion upwards from the grass roots in a democratic manner, is even more questionable. H. J. Hanham dismisses the claims of the Birmingham Liberals that not only the local associations but the National Liberal Federation itself, were truly democratic as 'transparent mendacity'.[1] There has been considerable discussion over the same general issue in the more recent past.[2]

However, the effects of interaction within party elites on their own attitudes and opinions are clearly important. To the faithful who participate, for instance, in the political education programmes run by some local Labour parties, or the 'Three-Way Contact Programme' of discussion directed for the constituencies by the Conservative Party Head Office, the party is itself an important reference group, providing reasoned support for strong convictions and attitudes, and offering the rewards of solidarity and approval to those who are content to absorb

[1] H. J. Hanham, *Elections and Party Management* (Longmans, 1959), p. 140.
[2] See particularly Robert McKenzie, *British Political Parties*, and L. Minkin, *The Labour Party Conference*, Unpublished PhD thesis, University of York.

their political coloration without undue intellectual stress from their immediate environment. It is not surprising that the more politically active will develop a more highly integrated and interrelated set of attitudes and opinions, more deeply internalized and less easy to shake loose. The competitive situation that preoccupies them provides an incentive to absorb the arguments and the claims that distinguish them favourably from the opposition. They can look regularly to national leadership for cues that will enable them to place new issues in the context of established perspectives and priorities. This aspect of organised political discussion is skilfully institutionalized within the Conservative Party in the response local parties receive if they submit to the Research Department of the Central Office summary reports of ward or constituency party discussions on the topics selected for the national programme.[1] Each group participating receives from a leading party spokesman in the relevant area a reflective response that is clearly based on a careful analysis of the discussion reports, picking up views that seem to contradict current party policy in a spirit of gentle but firm correction. In both parties, the extent to which discussion of this kind takes place varies considerably from local party to party, and in the case of the Tory Three-Way discussion programme there are considerable variations between broad geographical regions and between constituencies within regions. But however active the participation by active party members, there is no shortage of evidence that the process of political education into the more or less comprehensive political perspectives of the party leadership, national and local, is not carried much further by these means into the electorate at large. The more involved absorb their political perspectives through a process of identification with group norms. But only a small proportion of the public exposes itself to these pressures.

The extent to which the political perceptions of mass electorates lack the coherence and programmatic consistency that characterize the belief systems of the politically involved, has come as something of a surprise to sophisticated academics who have developed survey techniques to explore and interrelate the various dimensions of political belief and behaviour. In a seminal study, one of the authors of *The American Voter* has used the questionnaire measures of attitude and opinion, developed for the panel studies of the Survey Research Center at the University of Michigan, to examine the extent to which a diminishing level of information about politics across a national sample is associated with increasing fragmentation and loss of coherence among the various responses that

---

[1] There is considerable regional variation in participation in the 'Three-Way Contact Programme'. Between 1964 and 1965, the number of reports submitted by the 60 West Midlands Area constituencies went up from 62 to 155, whilst the number submitted by the 34 South Eastern Area constituencies went up from 77 to 468.

were elicited. As the salience of politics declines and political judgments are made on the basis of much-reduced information, even such an apparently elementary dimension for shaping attitudes as the liberal-conservative, or left-right continuum (habitually used by politicians and informed commentators) ceases to have any relevance or meaning for the respondents. Furthermore, quite apart from this kind of organizing dimension, Converse is able to show, by correlating responses to questions on different areas and comparing an elite with a cross-section sample, that related positions on different issue areas 'hang together' to a substantially greater degree for the sample of congressional candidates, despite the amorphous nature of the congressional parties. Once outside a relatively sophisticated 10 per cent in the national cross-section, attitudes cluster in issue areas, with very little connection perceived between them, and people tend to respond to questions in terms of the perceived interests of reference groups that are much more immediately salient to them than either of the political parties.[1] It is only for a decidedly small proportion of the population that the political parties are conceived of in terms of a relatively coherent and extensive set of attitudes—finding expression in relatively consistent and elaborated opinions on specific issues—towards social relationships and the goals of political action. For the great majority, and the British and American electorates are very similar in this respect, the parties figure in a different light.

The Berkeley survey directed by McClosky has produced a complementary picture. The party leaders in this sample taken from the delegates to the National Party conventions of 1956 seemed to have coherent and articulated perspectives, in which opinions on specific issues were related to underlying attitudes towards, for instance, the proper role of the government in intervening to regulate the national economy. These shared judgments were even in some respects at odds with any immediate electoral advantage. Of particular interest in this study was the discovery that, whilst the party followers in the sample could be distinguished from each other in terms of the direction of their responses to at least some sets of questions in the attitude and opinion questionnaires, it emerged that the *Republican* followers were in a sense better represented by the *Democratic* leaders than by their own nominal leadership, which seemed to retain attitudes perpetuated from an earlier period in the party's history. These attitudes were by then considerably eroded among traditional Republican supporters who had experience of the Depression and of Federal intervention in many areas of life since the Second World War. The consistent differences between the party leadership groups can be explained in terms of positive and negative reference groups and the kind of inducements to consistency discussed above:

[1] P. Converse, 'The nature of belief systems in mass public's', in D. Apter (ed.), *Ideology and Discontent* (Free Press, 1964).

'. . . [the party elites] comprise a smaller and more tightly knit group which is closer to the well-springs of party opinion, more accessible for indoctrination, more easily rewarded or punished for conformity or deviation, and far more easily affected, politically and psychologically, by engagement in the party struggle for office'.[1]

At the same time, this evidence of the isolation of the Republican leadership of the time from even its own following illustrates very well how the value of social-psychological explanations of the anchorage of attitudes and opinions in group interractions is contingent on the historical antecedents of the situation. The experience of the Depression and its consequences had drastically shaken the confidence of millions of people in the booming world of pre-Keynesian American capitalism. However crudely and inconsistently, popular perceptions of the functions of government had changed. But, for the Republican leadership that suffered the electoral consequences of that disaster, the Depression challenged a coherent and deeply internalized system of attitudes and beliefs, a powerful justificatory ideology that served to describe reality and provide interpretations within its own frame of reference for a chain of events that seemed to undermine its assumptions.[2] This ideology was powerfully resistant to change: alternative 'rational', or internally consistent, explanations were available: from the arguments of conservative economists laying the blame on the restrictive practices of the trade unions and the pressure of their wage demands, to allegations that socialistic and corrosive ivy-league economists were subverting the American system.[3]

A merely expedient resort to a revised set of appeals for electoral approval is not only inhibited by a diffuse association between a party and a state of affairs that is widely resented, particularly economic crisis or war; it is also restricted by what is recognized as conceivable by the leadership that will be forced to reorient its perceptions. The more deeply internalized and the more highly articulated the beliefs and attitudes of such an elite, the harder it will find the process of evolving an orientation that can effectively respond to an altered political universe and the more likely it will be to make serious errors of judgment about the political resources it can actually command.[4] A striking example that is directly

[1] H. McClosky, 'Issue conflict and consensus among party leaders and followers', The American Political Science Review, June 1960, pp. 406–27.

[2] See the analysis of this psychological process among extreme believers in L. Festinger, J. Riecken and S. Schachter, When Prophecy Fails (University of Minnesota Press, 1956).

[3] Keynes at Harvard, A Veritas Foundation Staff Study (New York 1960).

[4] Where a party's inherited ideology is, for the time being, preventing it from coming to terms with changing circumstances, the tendency of electorates to punish incumbents for the misfortunes that occurred when they were in

relevant to the history of post-war Republicanism is the support of the Goldwater candidacy by Republican managers, who, responding to the enthusiasm of local activists, made demonstrably wild assessments of a large popular following in tune with the political option that was represented by Barry Goldwater.[1]

In short, this kind of evidence on the cognitive and attitudinal structures of political decision-makers and their most active supporters, is highly ambiguous from the point of view of a discussion of rationality in the representative process. Warren Miller has merely elaborated, in the light of the detailed findings of the surveys, on the shrewd observation of Bryce with which this chapter began.

'The voter who is cognisant of few political objects, has few beliefs about politics, and has little or no structure relating his fragments of knowledge may respond sharply to a single new piece of information once it reaches him, but the response may be no more than random in its consequences for other attitudes and behaviours. The alert, informed, fully socialised political man will become aware of many more new pieces of information and will behave much more predictably, usually by incorporating them into his prior system of values and beliefs.'[2]

On the one hand, the informed, fully socialized political man commands the essential resources for rational behaviour, a high level of information and a trained sense of the interconnections between different areas of decision—the implications of expenditure on one set of priorities for the availability of resources demanded elsewhere, for example, or the likely consequences of a decision on some other group that belongs to the party coalition. He may be able to translate issues that many see in vague and emotive terms, into technically soluble problems, where the significant discussion is over the best means to an obviously desirable end. On the other hand, his political sophistication is not absolute. His command of information is organized by values that define the interests of the groups with which he identifies, the political coalitions and sacrifices they regard as feasible. The more highly socialized he is, the more internalized these values, the stouter the structure of the social reality he inhabits. Political leadership may be defined as the art of formulating responses to new threats and stresses in ways that do not undermine the basic values and beliefs that are held in common by a

---

power, whether they could be fairly held accountable or not, may contribute to the rationality of the process, whatever the punitive irrationality of the voters' intentions.

[1] P. Converse et. al., 'Electoral Myth and Reality: the 1964 Election,' The American Political Science Review, LIX, June 1965, pp. 321–37.

[2] W. Miller, 'Voting and Foreign Policy' in Rosenau (ed.), Domestic Sources of Foreign Policy (Free Press, 1967).

nation or by a political coalition, whatever the necessary objective changes in behaviour. But where the courage and imagination are lacking, or where objective changes have outpaced the ability to adapt to them, obsolescent belief systems may survive under the protection of institutional structures (as economic conservatism survived in the Republican Party) to influence decisions in ways that no longer seem rational in the light of changing demands made on the representative system.

A parallel example may be seen in the economic conservatism of the British Labour Party between the two world wars. We lack survey data for the period that might suggest how the mass following of the Labour Party would have responded to a different kind of leadership, particularly in the period of intense political activity around the General Strike and Great Depression. But the picture of the Labour leadership that emerges from the documentary evidence suggests a strong urge to inherit the mantle of the declining Liberals as a *national* party. It indicates also how thoroughly figures like Snowdon had absorbed the economic orthodoxies of that party, whose radical members, in the 'office of honorary family solicitors to the trade union movement', had been unable to conceive of a working-class movement emerging outside the Liberal Party.[1] Whether or not there would have been enough mass support for an energetic and genuinely socialist initiative.[2] or at least for a feasible non-socialist solution,[3] it is clear that the Labour leadership was constrained by a strong and generally shared acceptance of the legitimacy of traditional political institutions and by a conviction, symbolized by the talisman of the gold standard, that the security of the system itself depended on criteria of economic management that were already being questioned in other countries, without the benefit of a developed Keynesian theory. When Britain finally came off the gold standard in September 1931, the threat to the system was transformed into a model of simple rationality and, in Miliband's phrase, 'hardly a leaf stirred'. The Labour leadership, through its inability to take a confident initiative that would distinguish it from its disordered rivals, lost an opportunity to restructure the economically uninformed and inevitably superficial opinions of the bulk of its potential following and thereby to establish, as it has been struggling to do since, a general conviction of its effectiveness as a ruling party in the attitudes of the electorate at large.

Voter perspectives and rationality

For the bulk of the population, the reification of political parties is of a

[1] Hanham, op. cit., p. 328.
[2] R. Miliband, *Parliamentary Socialism* (Allen & Unwin, 1961).
[3] Robert Skidelsky, *Politicians and the Slump: The Labour Government of 1929–1931* (Macmillan, 1967).

very different kind. As organizations, and as a constant source of detailed cues on a range of items, they are remote, impinging intermittently and indirectly on day to day relationships at home or at work. Supposedly an essential means of organizing political perceptions, they cannot be said to perform that function very efficiently, or consistently. Analyses of the shifting of opinions over time in the mass followings of the parties show a volatility that suggests the importance of epidemic shifts of mood, to which coverage in the mass media might substantially contribute, infecting individuals who lack the involvement or information to connect many of their political judgments to their own more consistent orientations or to the proclaimed perspectives of their own party. For example, between the first and second interviews of the national sample surveyed by Butler and Stokes, only 39 per cent clearly maintained the same position on the issue of nationalization, a major dividing line between political elites. On the issue of nuclear weapons, the correlation between opinions expressed between the 1964 and 1966 interviews was only $+.38$, which was slightly larger than the correlation between the 1963 and 1964 interviews. For the small minority for whom a party is an immediate and salient reference group, divisions on these issues are part of the fabric of attitudes. For most of us, they float across the relationships we are involved in, and lack any connection with our direct experience.[1]

Uncertainty and indifference, rather than ignorance of the positions favoured by the parties, would seem to account for these fluctuations. The same respondents were clear how the parties divided on the well-established general issues of nationalization and the bomb, but any connection between their own responses and the party positions they correctly identified was random. Yet their attachment to one party or the other could survive these and other fluctuations without weakening. In a striking demonstration of the irrelevance of *structures* of opinions to party identifications, Butler and Stokes separated out of their sample those who responded with some stability, on a quite stringent test, to questions about issues put in the three interviews. Eliminating no less than 70 per cent of the full sample on the grounds that their opinions fluctuated from interview to interview, they correlated the responses of the remainder on a range of seven issues, in order to see if the structure of opinions at least in this subset of the sample echoed the structure of opinions among party elites. On these issues, according to informed opinion, the parties held discernably different opinions. The echo was there, but it was faint. 'People who opposed the recent level of immigration were more likely to be for the death penalty and against the power of the trade unions. Those who discounted the importance of the Monarchy were likely to accept nationalisation, oppose the Bomb, accept recent immigration,

[1] Butler and Stokes op. cit., pp. 178 and 181.

condemn hanging and the power of big business, and to be tolerant towards trade unions.'[1] However, the individual correlations are for the most part feeble.

Whatever is translated across the representative process from mass following to party leadership, it is certainly not a clear structure of commonly shared opinions on those current issues that seem to call for decision. Issue positions taken by party leaders have many determinants, from the mere pressure of partisan competition to a worthy urge to act rationally in the light of what is perceived as relevant evidence. Other pressures, which may or may not bear directly on the struggle for political power, and may or may not conduce to rationality of decision, emerge from the general public. The interaction this entails cannot realistically be described in terms of the considered individual judgments of the mythical ideal democrat we referred to earlier. Neither can it be described in terms of another familiar image, the old and much abused analogy of the pendulum swinging from left to right.

The analogy of the swinging pendulum is a thoroughly misleading one for a number of reasons. Not only does it impose on the individual voter an attitudinal dimension that only has meaning, in terms of the issues of the day, to a very few, but its application to aggregates of voters, in interpretations of election 'swing', tends to overlook the most difficult and interesting complexities. Net swing is of course vital to the election outcome and the transfer of power, but the final outcome is the result of two types of factor, each of which is far from simple in itself. One set of factors, which we now know to be far more important for the final outcome than is commonly realized, consists of the demographic changes that are constantly altering the constitution of the electorate, internal migration, boundary changes and so on, and variations in the birth and death rates, which add to and remove from the electorate layers of voters with very different characteristics.[2] The other set of factors consists of changes of attitude and opinion towards issues, leaders and parties themselves. The idea of the 'swing' suggests a oneway shift, but the reality may be vastly more confusing; some voters switch in one direction, some in another, or at a tangent to a minor party, for any number of reasons ranging from a possibly uncharitable association of recession in the industry they work in with the party that happens to be in power, to a dissatisfaction with the party they were born into, that has matured over a long period of time. Clearly a period of stable elections need not be the same thing as a period of electoral stability. There may be rapid crosscurrents under the bland surface of stable electoral competition.

The technical difficulties of analysing aggregate electoral data have

[1] Ibid., p. 199.
[2] See Butler and Stokes, op. cit., Ch. 12, for a very illuminating analysis of the impact of these factors.

contributed substantially to the survival of the simple notion of 'swing'. Where the only quantitative evidence consists of large blocks of votes in the constituencies, it is impossible to make more than simple assumptions about what is going on within those blocks of votes. Students of British electoral statistics are peculiarly handicapped in that the census areas in which other very useful data about the characteristics of the population are collected, only rarely correspond with the political unit of local and national constituencies. Furthermore, in our parliamentary elections, the ballots themselves as they come in from polling stations, are stirred into the general constituency stew, and the contributions of the different localities are lost in the general flavour of the popular will. American scholars, on the other hand, have been able to compare voting figures with useful census data that summarize a great deal of information about the life-style of local groups, such as figures on race, religion, national origin, occupation, and educational level. The units of comparison, right down to ward level, have been small enough to justify inferences about *what* forces are shifting electors in different elections.[1] Lee Benson has applied these techniques of aggregate analysis to much older census and electoral data from the Jacksonian period.[2] Lacking this kind of happy coincidence of data, it has been much harder to anatomize aggregate voting behaviour in the United Kingdom. Historians are by no means ignorant, of course, of local demography, but inferences from social conditions to political behaviour are bound to be generalized and tentative.[3] One consequence of this, which it is important to qualify to some extent, is a tendency to rely on 'class' as a general explanatory factor in voting behaviour. A general analysis leads to the unchallengable conclusion that class, however defined, is very highly associated with party affiliation in Great Britain. In the melting pot of American society, we are told, a rich variety of other factors are released into the political arena by the absence of hierarchical restraints which determine the stratified nature of European society. The determinants of British political behaviour are dull by comparison. 'Class is the basis of British party politics: all else is embellishment and detail.'[4] But it is not clear how much of an explanation the concept of class actually provides. It

[1] Louis Bean, for example, compared counties in the Middle West with differing concentrations of voters of German extraction, in order to explain variations in voting behaviour in the Roosevelt era. He was able to indicate roughly the extent to which Roosevelt's policy towards Germany affected voters whose national origin made this a salient issue. See L. Bean, *How to Predict Elections* (Knopf, 1948).

[2] L. Benson, *The Concept of Jacksonian Democracy* (Atheneum Press, 1958).

[3] H. Pelling, *The Social Geography of British Elections*, 1885–1910 (Macmillan, 1968). But see: *Census 1966, United Kingdom General and Parliamentary Constituency Tables*. HMSO, 1969.

[4] P. Pulzer, op. cit., p. 98.

may imply, first of all, a degree of polarization in the mass electorate which is similar to the polarization that lies implicit in the aggregating concept of electoral 'swing', the notion of a distribution of groups along a left-right continuum. But as we have seen, one important definition of such a continuum seems to be invalid and misleading. Secondly, the association between party identification and class, on any of its usual definitions, may be strong but is far from perfect. And thirdly, as a concept it does not stand on the same level as the more immediate determinants of the individual's life situation, his family and workplace environment and so on. Whether it is used as an objective description, classifying people in terms of their occupation, for instance, or as a category with which individuals subjectively identify, it assembles blocks of occupations and life styles, and it is by no means invariably clear which occupation should belong to which category. As a subjective, self-identification it is thoroughly ambiguous. From an analysis of questionnaires administered to a sample of factory workers in Luton, Goldthorpe and Lockwood have derived three distinct types of subjective image of class, each with different implications for the political perceptions of the individual, his aspirations, his general social reality. Awareness of class as a common life situation with common interests is, as a matter of historical fact, an intermittent and variable phenomenon. It is, in any event, mediated by the individual's experience of the social environment with which he is directly in contact.[1] It seems advisable to begin an analysis with the more immediate determinants and proceed later to a more general level. This is not simply a question of logical neatness, since a careless confusion of levels of analysis can affect argument on our main theme of political rationality in electoral choice.

Lee Benson's aggregate analysis of voting patterns in New York State in the Jacksonian era was designed to test a generally accepted assumption about electoral choice in that period, which derived from a class model of political conflict.[2] By anatomizing groups of voters in a systematic manner, he was able to show that—contrary to the assumptions of politicians at the time and of historians since—of far more importance to the electorate than identification with some generalized class image, was a sense of identification with a particular community, with its religious and ethnic character, its economic interests, and way of life. The act of voting was more a symbol of solidarity with one's own kind, and indeed of hostility towards other groups. From the point of view of those contemporaries who appear from the documentary evidence to have misperceived what was happening, the voters may have been irrational or perverse, but such a judgment employs narrow criteria for assessing the

[1] D. Lockwood, 'Sources of Variation in Working Class Images of Society', *Sociological Review*, Vol. 14, No. 3, November 1966.
[2] op. cit., especially Ch. VII.

nature of the political conflicts of the time. At other points in American, and certainly British, political history, a subjective identification with class has emerged in much stronger form, under the impact of industrialization on many occupational groups. It would be absurd to dispute that British society has been increasingly polarized along class lines since the reform bills of the last century.[1] But it remains true that aggregate electoral data can still be misleading. The great advantage of the survey is that it makes it possible to explore the psychological significance of this polarization and to distinguish components associated with class identifications from those associated with the more immediate environment of the individual, which mediate images of class. We can avoid assimilating everything to one broad explanatory category.[2] For a substantial proportion of the electorate, to be sure, political perceptions are reduced to a crude equation of a diffuse sense of class interest with a particular party. For many others, a generalized identification of class and party overlaps or cuts across an intermittent and selective interest in events in the political arena, as they impinge on what is seen as a more immediate group interest, or as the form in which they attract public attention—through the media and the tactics of politicians and opinion leaders—touches a chord in some underlying predisposition.

A subjective sense of identification with a class and with a party are related but not identical factors, which vary in importance over time and for different groups.[3] Taken together, in the setting of the British political culture with its broad consensus on the diffuse values of the system which cuts across party and class, they, as it were, summarize sets of attitudes that help maintain those institutions that provide the arena and rules of conflict and co-operation among groups and between them and government. Below lie the angularities of specific group identifications and compliance with group norms. It is at this more specific level that political allegiance is mobilized and changing circumstances are perceived and come to react sporadically and unevenly on attitudes and opinions. However simple the basic political alignments may appear, they are composed of a wide variety of orientations and priorities, many of them having little to do with a strictly economic self-interest. The demands

[1] For a descriptive survey of the evidence on class and party, see R. Alford, 'Class voting in the Anglo-American political systems', in S. M. Lipset and S. Rokkan, *Party Systems and Voter Alignments* (Free Press, 1969).

[2] For a detailed discussion of the concept of class and some of the questionable uses to which it has been put, see Gordon Leff, *History and Social Theory* (The Merlin Press, 1969), Ch. 9.

[3] Subjective identification with a class is affected by differences in life style apart from those associated with occupation. For instance, even in the lower manual grades, and more so in the intermediate, people who own or are buying their own homes are more likely to identify with the middle class. Butler and Stokes, op. cit., p. 72.

implicit in group identification, in all their complexity, are relevant to the process of representation and there are no *a priori* reasons for denying them a claim to rationality.[1]

Voting 'anomalies'

Recent survey evidence on three categories of elector illustrates the kind of interplay we are concerned with between subjective group identification, class identification, party identification, and different levels of response to political stimuli. The three categories are the 'working-class Tories', the 'affluent' working-class Labour voter, and university academics. All three groups seem to behave anomalously with respect to the class basis of politics.

The 'deferential' working-class Tory, who votes against his economic class interest, out of respect for the highly evolved capacity for leadership of those he deems to be his social superiors, is a prominent figure in contemporary political folklore. The rationality of his behaviour presumably varies according to the partisan position from which it is viewed. Bagehot's belief in a deferential nation[2] has always found support in the aggregate electoral figures, and, as McKenzie and Silver have pointed out,[3] the rationality of deference has been vigorously proclaimed by Conservative Party publicists. More recent survey studies have allowed the working-class Tory to speak for himself. In one sample, which included 320 working-class Tories,[4] 28 per cent of these believed that they would be better off under Labour, but still voted Conservative, and this position was associated in the questionnaire answers with approval of the party leadership on 'deferential' grounds, their special background, training and skills.

However, the careful analysis of the national sample by Butler and Stokes has differentiated the aggregate of working-class Tories still further. In the first place, as a proportion of the electorate they are not as significant as has often been supposed. The division, in this study, of occupational grades into two groups at the point between the skilled or supervisory non-manual and the lower non-manual was an innovation on the previous practice of market-research firms, which had combined these two grades, in spite of the clear tendency for the former group to identify with the middle class and the latter with the working class. This in itself affects the picture as far as class is concerned. The breakdown, in

---

[1] Pulzer seems to be using a narrower concept of rationality than the one we are attempting to explore here. 'Sociology in the main explains the reasons for long-term loyalty; psychology is more useful in explaining why some people change. Both emphasise the non-rational elements involved in political choice' op. cit., p. 113.

[2] W. Bagehot, *The English Constitution*, Ch. 8.

[3] op. cit. Ch. 2.

[4] E. A. Nordlinger, *The Working Class Tories* (Macgibbon & Kee, 1967).

terms of the proportions of the two collapsed occupational categories voting for either party reveals a smaller imbalance in apparently anomalous voting than other breakdowns of the figures have suggested. That is to say, the working class is more likely to vote Conservative than the middle class is to vote Labour, and the difference calls for explanation, but it is small enough to reduce the significance of the working-class Tory in the folklore.

		Occupational grade	
		I-III	IV-VI
Party	Conservative	a80%	b32%
self-image	Labour	c20%	d68%
		100%	100%

Difference, b−c=12%[1]

But it was also possible to use the questionnaire to get an indication of two broadly different sets of underlying beliefs and attitudes shaping perceptions of the structure of British society. For some, class was a salient reference group, but for others class was a relatively remote point of reference that failed to organize their more immediate perceptions of group interest. It is in *this* sub-category that working-class Conservative voting is highest.[2] Furthermore, it is not possible to infer from the responses to open-ended questions that there are underlying attitudes towards the structure of power that particularly distinguish the working-class Conservatives from other Conservative supporters. For the most part, the Conservative Party is supported for a widely diffused set of reasons. The deference voter exists, but in platoons rather than brigades. We may add that he presents one of the chicken-and-egg problems the survey cannot solve; the deferential attitude he expresses may be a consequence rather than a cause of his voting behaviour, which may be little more than a family heirloom whose original function has been forgotten. The expressions of deference may provide a rationale for ingrained habit.

A persuasive explanation of the working-class Conservative vote begins to emerge from the historical dimension built into the study. Breaking down the sample internally into age cohorts it is possible to compare, for each 'political generation', the difference between the equivalents of cells *b* and *c* in the fourfold table printed above. The difference drops decisively from 33 per cent for the pre-1918 age cohort to 16 per cent for the interwar and only 2 per cent for the 1945 cohort, before

[1] op. cit., p. 106.
[2] Ibid, p. 113.

an interesting *increase* to 6 per cent for the post-1951 generation.[1] Leaving aside for a moment the recent increase, it seems reasonable to see in these figures the impress of different substantive political experience during the most impressionable years of each of these political generations. For many older voters the Labour party simply failed to absorb or synthesize the various social identifications they grew into, failed, for instance, to make them respond to class as a general reference group or, in the case of local Conservatism in Lancashire, made a tardy impression on party attitudes that had strong historical roots in hostility to local Liberal mill-owners.[2]

The affluent working-class Labour voter presents a complementary anomaly. Electoral swings to the Conservative Party in the late 1950s introduced another figure into the folklore, a hypothetical working-class voter, whose increasing economic affluence was weaning him simultaneously into a middle-class and a Conservative state of development under the rubric of the elegant gallicism *embourgoisement*. The recent trend noted above towards more working-class Conservatism might be taken to support this inference from the aggregate figures. However, as Goldthorpe and Lockwood have shown, in their analysis of the 'critical case' of higher-paid workers in Luton factories where, if anywhere, one would expect to find *embourgoisement* under way, the process of partisan change is much less simply a matter of the interaction of economic affluence and class and party identification. If anything, their more affluent workers were keener Labour Party supporters. However, their evidence suggested a distinction between two broadly distinguishable kinds of orientation that lie behind Labour Party support. There is first the traditional kind of identification with the party, which would include both class-conscious communities, such as miners and dockers, who have strong historical grounds for a sense of working-class solidarity, and also the more socially conservative traditionalists. For these voters, being Labour supporters is just one of the aspects of identifying with their locality and community. Secondly there are the instrumentalists who are inclined, not exclusively, but to an appreciable extent, to make what is likely to be a more provisional identification with the Labour Party, associating it more with improvements experienced in the current economic position of the private family. In terms of our broad general framework, their orientations towards party as an institution are organized rather more at the level of opinion than of attitude.

Another finding of particular significance in this study is that the affluent workers who did vote Conservative were those whose immediate families, wife, parents and in-laws, could claim the most experience of

[1] ibid., p. 107.
[2] J. Mackintosh, 'Working Class Tories', a review of Nordlinger in *Socialist Commentary*, June 1967.

white-collar or intermediate jobs. Of respondents who lived in middle-
class housing areas, those with this kind of family connection with
middle-class occupations were much more likely to vote Conservative.
The upturn of working-class conservatism noted by Butler and Stokes
need not be inconsistent with this, since it can be shown that for the
electorate at large an increasing proportion of the wives of men in
manual occupations will have jobs in the middle-class occupational
category.

The university academics present a different kind of anomaly, since
we now have a middle-class group which, like all other groups, retains
the marks of its largely middle-class origins and early socialization, but
nonetheless deviates from the position its class would indicate.[1] The
extent of the anomaly can be seen from a comparison Halsey and Trow
make between a set of Gallup Poll figures from a national sample, and
their own figures from the sample of university teachers, comparing
percentage differences by class, for support of the three parties.

Party support:	Class			University teachers
	upper	middle	working	
	%	%	%	%
Conservative	77	65	33	38
Labour	9	22	53	45
Liberal	14	13	14	15

The university teachers, an undeniably middle-class group, distribute
their support to the parties very much more like the working class. It is
as true for university teachers as for any other group that they do not
arrive at their political choices through the travail of pure and private
reasoning. (It is also the case that they are as a group no more active or
interested in politics than middle-class people generally.) Further
breakdowns of the questionnaire data throw some light on the patterns
of group identification and compliance with group norms that are taking
place. For instance, the authors show that there are substantial differences between academics in different subjects, and these differences remain even when the analysis 'controls' for social origins, another
factor which might influence attitudes. Thus 70 per cent of the social
scientists describe themselves as Far Left or Moderately Left, whilst
only 45 per cent of those teaching medicine or technological subjects so
describe themselves. The social scientists seem much more responsive to
the traditionally Left-Liberal political culture of the universities, and it
is suggested that this is partly a result of the historical orientation of these

[1] See the forthcoming study, *British Academics* (Faber), by A. H. Halsey and
Martin Trow. The information cited here comes from their draft of Ch. VII.

disciplines in this country and party a result of the free-floating status of the social scientist, whilst scholars in the technical or medical fields have professional reference groups that lie to a considerable extent outside the university world and in very different political climates.

The distribution of attitudes and opinions, the patterns and variations in intensity of reference group affiliations, are nothing if not complex. A specific issue, like the development of comprehensive schools, will find an immediate and attentive public in the university teachers, for whom it is a matter of direct concern, besides embodying problems that touch on underlying attitudes towards the social structure, egalitarian norms and deeply internalized professional standards. For slightly different constellations of reasons it will affect other groups, and may provide the basic impetus for organized political initiatives that will affect politicians and civil servants. Elsewhere in the party coalition it may have very little resonance indeed. It may even, as was in fact the case over comprehensives, find relatively attentive support in the general following of the opposing party, in spite of the initial principled opposition of Conservative party leaders.

Different networks of publics, voters whose attention is held by specific issues, and who may or may not have the organizational resources to express their interest coherently or persistently, are constantly engaged with the institutions that make and carry out decisions. In the short run, responses to current issues of uneven salience to different groups may have little effect on basic identification with class and party. But historical developments, the errors and successes of political elites imperceptibly reshuffle alignments and shift perceptions at the broader, generalizing level. We can return to this more long-term and viscous process of change, after discussing the ongoing politics of organized attentive publics.

4

The Pressure-group Universe

The time is long past when pressure groups were regarded as being virtually identical with 'sinister' or 'vested' interests whose machinations were invariably contrary to the public interest or general will. Few serious students of society now accept Rousseau's view 'that there should be no partial society within the state, and that each citizen should think only his own thoughts'.[1] Instead one finds that pressure groups are commonly regarded not only as normal phenomena whose activities must be included in any full account of democratic (and other kinds of) politics, but also as being virtually necessary components of any free or democratic system. It is not merely that pressure groups are seen to thrive under conditions of political liberty, as James Madison asserted of factions;[2] many are seen, rather, as necessary conditions for the survival of political liberty.[3]

Leaving aside for the present the more enthusiastic normative claims, there remain important ways in which pressure groups may contribute crucially to the processes and principles which characterize modern democratic systems and by reference to which the existence and activities of pressure groups are sometimes defended.

On many aspects of government, ranging from decisions on major policy to the minutiae of administration, the only significant public will consist of one or more pressure groups. It may therefore be claimed that

[1] *The Social Contract*, Book II, Ch. III. But see also R. Titmuss, *The Irresponsible Society* (Fabian Society, 1960), in which some echoes are clearly detectable.

[2] *The Federalist Papers*, 1787, No. X: 'Liberty is to faction what air is to fire, an aliment without which it instantly expires'.

[3] See, for example, S. E. Finer, *The Anonymous Empire* (Pall Mall, second edition, 1966), p. 113, where he argues that, without 'the Lobby', the ruling party would be 'a rigid and ignorant tyranny' and the civil servants 'a rigid and stupid bureaucracy'. See also, B. Crick, *In Defence of Politics* (Weidenfeld & Nicolson, 1962) especially Ch. I; J. Blondel, *Voters, Parties and Leaders* (Penguin Books, 1963), Ch. 6; G. Sartori, *Democratic Theory* (Praeger, 1965), especially pp. 401–2; and the modern literature of pluralism, of which influential representatives include S. M. Lipset, *Political Man* (Doubleday, 1960) and W. Kornhauser, *The Politics of Mass Society* (Routledge & Kegan Paul, 1960).

the process of discussion sometimes depends entirely upon pressure groups and at all times is likely to depend upon them to some extent.[1] They may thus constitute 'public opinion' on certain issues, and, to use an Aristotelian metaphor, serve as the clearest indicators of 'where the shoe pinches'. In one of the more discreet sides of their work, as in the face-to-face examination of problems and issues by official advisory committees, pressure groups may contribute also to the 'search for rationality' in policy making.[2] Taking both their more public and their more confidential activities together, they may be seen collectively as a system of functional representation supplementing, and possibly even supplanting in importance, the formal constitutional system of territorial representation.[3] No discussion of representation is therefore complete without account being taken of pressure groups. This judgment applies also to any discussion of the nature of opposition in general, and in any particular regime. Indeed, as we shall argue below, pressure groups derive much of their influence and status from their capacity successfully to oppose governments, while what is opposed, by which groups, and by what means, are among the salient features which distinguish different political systems. Finally, it may be argued, legitimate popular power, whether asserted by a majority or, especially, by a minority striving to become or persuade the majority, is likely to be nebulous without the opportunity to mobilize and organize, including the formation of pressure groups, and to create clienteles or attentive publics.

With none of the claims stated in the previous paragraph do we wish directly to quarrel. But, if they are taken as statements of fact about British politics, or about any country's politics for that matter, then it must be pointed out that they are not necessarily nor invariably true. To show why this is so we must survey the pressure group system.

Terminology

By 'pressure group' we mean, simply, any organized group which attempts to influence government decisions without seeking itself to exercise the formal powers of government.[4] The latter part of the defini-

---

[1] Thus R. T. McKenzie has concluded that 'pressure groups . . . are a far more important channel of communication than parties for the transmission of political ideas from the mass of citizenry to their rulers', in his 'Parties, Pressure Groups and the British Political Process', *Political Quarterly*, XXIX, 1958. For a good brief discussion of this impact on legislation, see S. A. Walkland, *The Legislative Process in Great Britain* (Allen & Unwin, 1968), Chs. III and IV.

[2] PEP, *Advisory Committees in British Government* (Allen & Unwin, 1960), pp. 112–13.

[3] See Samuel H. Beer, *Modern British Politics* (Faber, 1965), and especially the definitions of functional and territorial representations on pp. 71–3.

[4] This is virtually identical with other widely accepted definitions. See, for example, H. Eckstein, *Pressure Group Politics* (Allen & Unwin, 1960), pp. 9–11.

tion is usually intended to distinguish a pressure group from a political party or conspiratorial group, while the stress on organizations distinguishes it from a mob or other spontaneous collection of individuals. Again in line with established usage, we do not mean to imply, by labelling an organization as a pressure group, that its sole or even principle aim is to influence government; we mean no more than that it does, on occasion, pursue that aim.

Disputes about terminology are as often fruitless as not, but in this case it is necessary to say why we reject another prevalent label, that of 'interest group'.[1] The trouble with this label as we see it lies in the risk of confusion with other established usages. On the one hand 'interest groups' are frequently contrasted with 'attitude', 'promotional' or 'cause' groups, as a means of classification within the general population of pressure groups. Even as such the term is open to objection, but it has an established reference to those pressure groups whose members are linked by a shared interest of, normally, an economic or occupational kind; it is best retained exclusively for this use.[2] On the other hand, the term is liable to confusion with the notion simply of an interest, in the sense in which that word was used in, for example, the Philadelphia Convention of the American Founding Fathers, or the nineteenth-century debates on suffrage extension in both the USA and Britain. We feel that it is still useful to be able to talk of the commercial, landed, church, business, or labour *interest*, in the sense of an identifiable and important section of the community whose responses and welfare no government dare ignore, without any necessary implication that it is organized or has a single spokesman or pressure group to represent it. Indeed, it is important to distinguish an interest (in this admittedly slightly old-fashioned sense) from the variety of pressure groups which may be formed from its members—there are, for example, too many conflicting perceptions and priorities within the broad interests of business and labour for it to be sensible to refer to either as a pressure group—if only because, as we will argue below, an important feature of the pressure-group *system* is that, on certain issues, otherwise mutually antagonistic groups will form a coalition based on their common growth from a single interest.

Professor Finer prefers to talk of 'the lobby' to refer to the universe of groups and associations which try to influence government. This label

---

It is also almost identical with what S. E. Finer, op. cit., pp. 2–5, means by a 'lobby'.

[1] As in the title of W. Ehrmann (ed.), *Interest Groups in Four Continents* (University of Pittsburgh, 1958).

[2] On this distinction, see, for example, F. G. Castles, *Pressure Groups and Political Culture* (Routledge & Kegan Paul, 1967), pp. 2–3, and Eckstein, loc. cit.

is, however, open to the objection that outside the USA it is a slightly eccentric term, while inside the USA it tends to have too narrow a connotation, being primarily associated with that sector of pressure groups activities which focus on the federal or state legislatures.[1] But, of the various possibilities, it is probably the most satisfactory alternative to 'pressure group', if one is needed. Finer rejects 'pressure group' because, in essence, the term 'implies that some kind of sanction will be applied if a demand is refused, and most groups, most of the time, simply make requests or put up a case . . . [and secondly] . . . even groups which *do* use pressure do not do so all the time'.[2] As a descriptive statement this is unchallengeable; but it less adequate as an aid to explanation. In particular it side-steps the underlying question of why some people's groups are heeded and others are not, of how some, and only some, have come to be included in the charmed circle of those whose views are always sought by governments, or of how a new group comes to be recognized as being worth taking seriously. Part of the answer to this kind of question is that a group is recognized as representing some legitimate and established section of society. But another, and crucial part of the answer, is that the government discovers that it wants something from the group in question—either co-operation or the ending of non-co-operation—and can only or most readily obtain it by paying attention to the group's demands or wishes. Underlying the continuing relationship between group and government, this is to say, is at least the possibility of sanctions or pressure, however gentlemanly, of the kind so well described by Professor Finer with reference only to what he considers to be exceptional circumstances.[3] The point is that the absence of overt or continuing pressure no more establishes the insignificance of pressure than the absence of war demonstrates the irrelevance of armed forces to the continuance of peaceful diplomatic relations between states.

Heterogeneity

At first sight the world of pressure groups can be bewildering, so great is the variety of groups and activities. Apart from their shared concern to persuade others there seems little in common between, for example: 'highbrow' literary campaigns by the associations for the reform of the laws on homosexuality, abortion, divorce or obscenity; ramblers' associations resolutely hiking and petitioning local authorities to keep open traditional rights of way in rural England; earthy yeoman farmers

[1] One is therefore tempted to suggest that pressure groups which focus on the administration be labelled 'the Ante-Room'.

[2] S. E. Finer, op. cit., p. 3.

[3] op. cit., pp. 125–33. And see the general conclusion of J. D. Stewart, *British Pressure Groups* (Oxford, 1958), that campaigns in, or directed towards, the House of Commons are designed largely to secure recognition for a group by the permanent administration.

(and agricultural businessmen) engaged, through the National Farmers' Union, in tough annual bargaining over prices and subsidies with their sponsoring Whitehall Ministry; rioting by militant associations of social or religious bigots in Belfast; gentlemanly public and private attempts by civic societies to persuade local councillors of the cash and prestige value of urban aesthetics. Nevertheless, some attempt must be made to order the field.

There are numerous ways, first, by which pressure groups may be classified. One of the commonest we have already referred to: the distinction between interest, sectional, spokesman or functional groups on the one hand, and, on the other, promotional or cause groups. The precise terminology and meaning varies, but the general import is the same, and significant. For there is an important difference between those groups which speak for a recognizable section or interest in a society, whether it be an industry, a trade union, a profession, council-house tenants, or surtax payers, and those which exist to promote a particular ideal or 'cause'. Membership of the former derives largely from those in a particular, relatively clearly definable, location within the social or economic structure in virtue of which they are likely to be similarly affected by events (including government action or inaction). In principle, moreover, the total number of people in that location is discoverable, so that it is not obviously nonsensical for a group to say that it represents a certain percentage of those for whom it claims to speak. By contrast, there is no comparable clientele (other than the whole body of citizens) for promotional groups which must attract members because of a consensus of opinion on a specific issue (such as the location of a new London airport) or because they share a more general disposition (such as the complex of anxieties about nuclear weapons which first brought many people into the Campaign for Nuclear Disarmament), and not primarily, if at all, on the basis of their sharing certain other socially identifiable characteristics. This distinction can be important in terms of the methods objectives and relationships with governments likely to be sustained by the two types of group. But we doubt whether it is caught in an equally satisfactory way by all the pairs of terms in common use, or entirely satisfactorily by any.

Of the labels mentioned, 'spokesman' is the least meaningful in that all leaders claim to speak for their group, and one is always prompted to ask who or what kind of group they in fact speak for. The least satisfactory dichotomy is that between interest and attitude groups. Attitudes, as we have seen in a previous chapter, vary widely with respect to their organization, specificity, cognitive content and linkages; different causes may therefore be supported by individuals with very different kinds and sets of attitudes. It is therefore preferable to stress the object (cause) or the activity (promotion of a cause) in the label. But the main objection to the interest-attitude distinction is that it suggests a sharper distinction than is warranted. Even leaving out of account any empirically discoverable prevalence of certain attitudes among members of particular sections or interests, the distinctiveness is blurred by the extent to which interests and sections are in part defined and identified with reference to the attitudes, beliefs and perspectives of 'their' members and of society at large. Indeed, one purpose of pressure-group activity may be merely to alert members and non-members to the existence of interests that opinion-leaders believe should be salient to the particular groups they represent. The objection being raised here is not, however, that one wants to sharpen the distinction, but that the labels should more clearly indicate its relativity while still preserving it. Since 'functional' describes only some of the important non-promotional groups, and 'sectional' carries overtones of disapproval as well as seeming too objective, we are forced to suggest our own terminology. We therefore recommend that promotional groups be contrasted with 'formal role groups', meaning by the latter groups whose members are brought together initially at least by virtue of some shared role(s), whether it be that of parent, teacher, textile worker, public employee, company director or gnome of Zürich.

The principal advantage of this term is that it will be obvious to anyone who knows what 'formal role' means[1] that a formal role group is socially defined and is not independent of prevailing expectations and beliefs. Furthermore, it will be obvious that which roles are considered to be important at any given time and place is also a function of the social and cultural environment. At the same time, a role group also has a finite membership and can encompass innumerable sub-categories, including those whose utility is already established. In particular, it is clear that the genus formal role group includes such well-known species as producer and consumer groups, the professions, civic groups, churches, educational and cultural groups.[2] It also does full justice to the notion of a functional group (while still having a wider and more suggestive meaning) to the extent that, as a matter of fact, those groups who perform roles which are crucial to the economic process will be among the most important and effective of pressure groups.

Effectiveness
With respect to all types of pressure group, it may next be asked what factors affect their likelihood of success and their general mode of opera-

[1] Role has been defined as 'a named social position characterized by a set of (a) personal qualities and (b) activities, the set being normatively evaluated to some degree both by those in the situation and others'. *A Dictionary of the Social Sciences* (Tavistock, 1964), p. 609.
[2] See S. H. Beer, op. cit., pp. 319–51, and the classification suggested by S. E. Finer, op. cit., pp. 6–18.

tions. Broadly and tritely speaking, a group will succeed to the extent
that a government wishes to, or *must*, heed it, and is therefore open to
persuasion. If a government wishes to heed a group, then the element
of pressure is overlaid. This situation arises not infrequently; governments constantly require advice, information and other kinds of assistance from outsiders, the assistance including, on occasion, the exercise
of authority for public ends.[1] Many groups come into being largely to
serve some public purpose defined by government. For such groups,
persuasion may be largely a matter of evidence and argument; of
educating governments, since there is agreement about the purpose and
nature of the consultation. But for these groups if circumstances change
—and for other groups—other kinds of persuasion, direct and indirect,
and ranging from less logical forms of argument to threatened insurrec-
tion, may be invoked. Essentially, various forms of actual or potential,
active or passive, non-co-operation[2] may be, or seem to be, the only
course open to a group which does not receive the hearing to which it
feels entitled. It must be remembered, too, that experienced politicians
and administrators will normally be fully aware of the pressures to which
they might be subjected (and of the counter-pressures they can themselves mobilize) if discussions fail to secure agreement or if they choose
to ignore the wishes or demands of a group. The absence of pressure may
therefore be of little significance—it could, conceivably, mean either that
the potential pressure is so great that it need not be applied, or that the
aggrieved group has no available leverage; no blanket judgment is
possible, except that, other things being equal, the persuasive power and
status of any given group is a function of the size of problem which it
would create for government by its non-co-operation (and of the likelihood that it would in fact withhold its co-operation). And this is, in
the long run, as true of those groups whom governments seek out as of
those who thrust themselves forward.

More comprehensively, the effectiveness (persuasive power) of any
group will be a function (still subject to the qualification that other things
are equal, a qualification to be 'unpacked' later in this chapter) of the
resources it controls,[3] its ease of access to decision-makers, and the skill
and knowledge with which it exploits these.

[1] Britain during World War II, and the USA during the early years of the New
Deal, saw great administrative responsibilities being virtually conferred upon
Trade Associations, for example. In Britain it is also difficult to say whether such
bodies as the General Medical Council or the Law Society are public or private.
See S. A. Walkland, op. cit., Ch. IV.

[2] Including, of course, ceasing to give a government what it wants in the
way of information or advice, i.e. 'not speaking'. See S. H. Beer, op. cit., p. 331.

[3] In the sense of the word 'resource' used by, for example, R. A. Dahl,
Modern Political Analysis (Prentice-Hall, 1963), and *Who Governs?* (Yale
University Press, 1964), it is equivalent to 'sources of power'.

Any list of the major sources of political strength, and not of strength for pressure groups alone, must begin with control over the means of force and violence. The army was clearly politically active over the Irish Question in 1914, and the views of the police undoubtedly delayed the abolition of the death penalty for civil offences after the Second World War. Otherwise, however, outside immediate 'professional' issues, the armed and police forces in Britain seem to accept a non-political role. Generally, too, organized 'unofficial violence' is exceptional in recent political history outside Northern Ireland. There is no eternal 'embargo' upon the exploitation of force as a domestic political resource, however, as mounting racial tension or the increasing militancy of radical youth may serve to warn us. It cannot therefore be passed over without mention.

Of much greater and more obvious significance in modern industrialized society, particularly in a 'growth-oriented' age, is control of the means of production, distribution and exchange as one does not need to be a Marxist to appreciate.[1] The controllers of such resources obtain political leverage both directly and indirectly. They gain indirect leverage to the extent that the wealth and income derived from their economic activities, and especially from industry and commerce (the principal generators of private wealth in modern societies) can be used to purchase influence or mobilize other resources.[2] The direct forms are both more numerous and, in the short run, probably more important. The bargaining instruments available to those who hold key positions in the economy—and their number is legion, even if they are not all relevant in every context—are both multiple and potentially strong. Among them are: actual or threatened withdrawals of labour, which may be important not only in a 'general strike' situation or on the part of virtual public employees like doctors and schoolteachers, but even when the immediate target is 'private'; refusal actively to co-operate with a government policy, as adopted by the iron and steel industry when resisting its nationalization in 1950; 'crises of confidence' in the City of London; reluctance to devote energies to export markets or to invest resources in

[1] If evidence be wanted, it is necessary only to look through any standard work on pressure groups and to compare the space and attention given to economic and especially producer groups, in comparison with that devoted to other kinds of formal role or promotional ones.

[2] Including organization, skill, information and informal access to decision-makers (see below) as well as publicity and an easier road to public office. The importance of the last two must not be exaggerated, as it often is in popular discourse, in the British context; some relevant evidence may be found in, e.g., R. Rose, *Influencing Electors* (Faber, 1967), A. Ranney, *Pathways to Parliament* (Macmillan, 1965), and W. L. Guttsman, *The British Political Elite* (Macgibbon & Kee, 1963). One must not overlook, either, the role of financial dependence by the Labour Party upon the Trade Unions and by the Conservatives upon business.

particular regions or activities; or resistance to reorganization in industry, whether it be of work habits or of basic structure. It is, of course, true that many of these instruments are used with no political or pressure purpose in mind. But they may be invoked in order to persuade, and even when not being used 'with intent', the effect may be the same—the government will have to reconsider, if not necessarily change, its behaviour: 'all governments are forced to work within the limits which such anticipated reactions impose upon them.'[1] The fact is that conscious and overt pressure is but one end of a continuum which includes these 'twilight' activities (as Finer calls them) and the other end of which consists of, for example, 'straight' business decisions about prices, products, or investments, purely internal decisions about union organization, or 'autonomous' decisions whether or not to expand on the part of the universities, the effects of which are, in the future, to open or close particular policy options. No discussions of pressure groups make sense, particularly in the economic sphere, which does not relate pressure politics to other, even if 'accidental', manifestations of the ability to shape or influence government policies.

The better organized any group is, the more effective it is likely to be, whatever its membership or purpose. The classic instance is, of course, the transformation of industrial relations and, in time, of almost the entire social fabric, brought about by the successful organization of the labour force into trade unions. In the larger industrially developed societies today it often, indeed, seems impossible to accomplish any public purpose, and an increasing number of private ones, except through some organization or another. Organization must therefore itself be counted a resource.

Closely related to organization, and especially dependent upon it, is mere number—the greater proportion of the population (relative either to the society as a whole or to the members of a particular category thereof) enrolled, other things again being equal, the greater the group's impact. Even unorganized, numbers are a resource—as such things as the importance of civilian morale in war-time testifies.

Ideas and beliefs obviously have a place in any account of pressure groups, if only because the object of pressure is often to change them—and not only in the case of promotional groups. They must also be seen as a resource, in three different ways. Certain groups, of which churches are the chief historical examples, are organized round a particular set of beliefs. Any group, secondly, gains in cohesion, and hence in strength, where there is a sense of mission, a distinctive rationale or a strong sense of commitment on the part of the members. Thirdly, a group will be stronger or weaker depending on whether it is swimming with or against

---

[1] S. E. Finer, op. cit., p. 132; and for examples of most of these tactics, see his general discussion on p. 128 et seq.

the tide of socially accepted standards and beliefs. To stand for something which 'no decent respectable citizen' would publicly oppose, like the prevention of cruelty to animals in Britain, is a clear asset which groups will seek to acquire, even if only by paying large sums to public relations consultants.[1] To be or appear legitimate is an important political resource. (It is worth remembering, however, that in pressure groups as in political parties,[2] the leadership will have more clearly articulated attitude and beliefs about its functions and purposes than in general will its public following. For some followers, identifying with the pressure group will be little more than a matter of compliance with a group norm which is maintained, in part, by the organizational efforts of the leadership.)

Another important resource is the control of scarcity. Whether it is skill, information or a commodity which is in scarce supply (i.e. in relation to the demand for it), its controller(s) have a strong bargaining position. A resource whose importance is often exaggerated is the means of communication, but if one thinks of all the means of communication —of people and things as well as of messages, i.e. of 'lines' as well as the 'media'—then it is clearly of great significance as the control approaches a monopoly.

Finally, one must include, as a possible resource, control over or the possession of access to the decision-makers: witness the power of confidants, private secretaries, the mistresses of great men, and the like, as well as the value of obtaining (and peddling) inside information.[3]

Access to decision-makers is of such importance for pressure-group effectiveness, however, that it must be treated as a category separate from resources. For lack of it, a group may be driven to disaffection from the political system, and if control of significant resources is allied to the denial of access, the situation is ripe for rebellion.[4] But the precise channels of access are what matter in less extreme circumstances, and it is upon them that we wish to focus.

Of these, the most obvious and the most reliable are the formal channels built into the structures of government. These include, of course, election and/or appointment to formal office. In any system certain kinds of individual, or individuals from certain social categories or groups, are more likely than others to be chosen; groups which have a significant

[1] It is worth reflecting on the difference between opposing the 'dilution' of labour on the shop-floor and restricting entry into a profession in order to 'maintain professional standards'.

[2] See Ch. 3 above.

[3] On the usefulness to the commercial television pressure group in the 1950s, of access at Cabinet level, see H. H. Wilson, *Pressure Group: The Case of Commercial Television* (Secker & Warburg, 1961), and Ch. 5 below.

[4] The converse situation, of access combined with impotence, provides a definition of the pure courtier.

say in this selection process or have some of their leaders or members selected have gained formal access. So, too, have those who are invited into consultations with the government or on to the 500 or so significant advisory committees with which the administration surrounds itself.[1] Under the same heading of formal channels one should also, probably, include the political parties which tend to have their own special clientele among pressure groups, consisting of those groups on which they are particularly dependent for support, those whose aims they find congenial, or those who happen to supply the party with members.[2] Any good modern text on British government gives some account of the groups and sections which obtain formal access, so we will not elaborate here.[3] Too much must not be made, however, of statistics about, for example, the associational links of MPs. Many MPs only form these links *after* they are elected and in accordance with their own political preferences and concerns, and few, if any, MPs see themselves as mandated to follow an association's 'line' (even when in fact they do so)—we are saying no more than that they provide points of access and that, in so far as any group secures formal access to decision-making, it may be able to dispense with the more blatant forms or 'pressure' or 'lobbying'.[4]

The relationships between government and groups in society implied in the notion of access are not of course permanent or immutable, though they tend to develop expectations and vested interests that are extraordinarily resistant to change. Indeed, it is very relevant to the analysis of the rationality of political behaviour, the dimensions of which we

[1] PEP, *Advisory Committees in British Government* (Allen & Unwin, 1961), estimated that some 500+ out of the more than 800 advisory committees were worthy of serious study.

[2] The Trade Unions' connections with the Labour Party are the best known: but the interconnections of both with CND are also instructive. See respectively, Martin Harrison, *The Trade Unions and the Labour Party since 1945* (Allen & Unwin, 1960); and F. Parkin, *Middle Class Radicalism* (Manchester University Press, 1968), especially Ch. 6. H. H. Wilson, op. cit., provides a fascinating account of the exploitation of the Conservative Party by the commercial television group, as well as of the use of pressure group tactics and organization by the Conservative Central Office; he suggests, too, that this case is not atypical of inner-Party policy making. These cases are discussed further in the next chapter.

[3] But, in particular, see W. L. Guttsman, op. cit., R. K. Kelsall, *The Higher Civil Service* (Routledge & Kegan Paul, 1955), the table of MPs' occupations, etc., given in D. Butler and A. King, *The British General Election of 1966* (Macmillan, 1966), and the earlier volumes of the Nuffield series on post-war elections, and S. H. Beer, 'The Representation of Interests in British Government', *American Political Science Review*, September 1957.

[4] Which may be one reason why, until comparatively recently, pressure groups were not generally acknowledged to form part of the British scene. On the other hand, the greater occupational homogeneity of the US Congress and the extent to which membership of Congress amounts to a more full-time occupation than being an MP, combined with the different constitutional position, made 'lobbying' more necessary, given the lack of direct and formal group access.

distinguish in the next chapter, to remember that conflict over the formal structure of access may be more immediately important to a pressure group than simply urging its recommendations through whatever channels are currently open to it. Many of a pressure group's problems might dissolve if, say, two Ministries were amalgamated or a new one created, or if a committee, such as the Maud Committee on Local Government, could be persuaded to adopt a particular principle over the reorganization of local authorities.[1]

Information about who benefits from the formal routes of access is important in another way: it provides data from which one may begin to draw a map of the informal routes. In Britain, where such notions as 'the establishment', the 'old boy network', and 'the grapevine' are commonplaces of political discussion, few people need to be persuaded that these informal channels are or may be important, and no one would deny it who had any first-hand political experience at any level.[2] Informal access is an inevitable aspect of social interaction. On occasion, of course, such interaction may be a product of chance or purely personal factors. It also tends to arise out of official relationships. But it is facilitated, and its probability increased, between people with a 'common background', i.e. shared attitudes or membership of some social grouping which they perceive as significant. Such interaction, where it is between people 'in' government and others who are not, constitutes informal access. Among the more important channels, it follows, will be common membership (on the part of governors and outsiders) of family, club, educational establishment, society or association, committee, and, at the limit of significance, social class.[3] Common membership does not, of course, necessarily carry with it political agreement, mutual friendship, conspiracy or even unqualified acceptance, although sometimes it does. But it does facilitate understanding (and, hence, on occasion, mutual antagonism) and does enlarge the possibilities of communication.[4]

[1] See, for an interesting case-study, F. Smallwood, *Greater London: The Politics of Metropolitan Reform* (Bobbs-Merrill, 1965). The extent to which powerful group attitudes may identify a salient substantive issue in an apparently 'neutral' organizational problem is clearly brought out in his account of the response to proposed changes in London's government on the part of four role-groups: the teachers, the doctors, the architects and planners, and the Welfare and Children's Service.

[2] If hard evidence is demanded, one reference should suffice, to the *Report* of the inquiry into alleged leaks of information about the increased Bank Rate in 1957 (Cmnd. 350 of January 1958).

[3] To the extent that interaction tends to take place more readily within class boundaries, partly because—especially in a highly class-aware society like the British (particularly among the older generation)—class insignia seem to aid evaluation and sympathy and to include, in some degree, 'speaking the same language'.

[4] And, in our view, this is the only significance which can safely and reliably

One other basis of access must be noted: known control of an important political resource. Automatic access is not, of course, assured—groups have often to demonstrate that they in fact have bargaining power, just as, when this is granted, they may have to establish their respectability. The usual qualification—that other things are equal—holds here too. But if it is made, then it is clear, as students have recently discovered in their dealings with university authorities, that power produces access eventually.

To round off the story, even in outline, we must look at some of the more important contextual limitations upon pressure group influence. Only then can we return to the question of the role of pressure groups in a democratic system. But first we wish to call attention to one basic conclusion which follows from the discussion so far: inequality of access and in the control of resources, and hence of the opportunity to exert pressure on government, is neither accidental nor the result of a deliberate conspiracy of the wicked or the selfish; it is unavoidable in a complex society with an elaborate division of labour operating in a world of which a central attribute is scarcity (of time, effort and ability, as well as of goods); the degree and importance of the inequality will vary, but not the fact of it.

The political culture, government, and the pressure-group system

It is obvious that pressure groups do not 'run the show'—campaigns fail and group spokesmen constantly lament their frustrations. Rarely, if ever, is a policy adopted or rejected *merely* because of pressure-group activities—for all that one needs to know which group(s) support or oppose what proposal if one is to understand the issues, or appreciate what is at stake.

One limit upon pressure groups is their sheer plurality; pursuing competing purposes, they check one another. But this is by no means universally restricting in the way in which a large number of firms guarantee one another's 'good behaviour' in the classical economic model of perfect competitive markets. By no means every group has its anti-group, and even if it did, for a perfect 'pressure market' to exist, they would need to be of substantially equal effectiveness, and there would need to be an anti-group on every issue. But it is patently not the case that, as it were, for every conspiracy to raise prices,[1] there is a conspiracy to lower them. The effectiveness of any particular group is also limited

---

be attached to many sociometric analyses of decision-makers. That it is unsafe, e.g., to draw conclusions about the *political beliefs* of civil servants from their class and educational backgrounds was surely made clear by the dramatic espionage of Burgess, McLean and Philby.

[1] Adam Smith's view of the outcome whenever businessman meets businessman.

by the fact that its members may belong to other groups, and will in any case probably feel only a conditional loyalty to it. But how strong a limit this is will depend on, among other things, the centrality of the group's purposes to its members' lives and the centrality of a particular issue to the group's purposes.[1] It is nevertheless important to remember that pressure groups are not necessarily internally homogeneous and that many have, to adapt the old jingle, 'other pressure groups upon their backs to bite them.'[2]

These limits, broadly speaking, operate within the pressure-group system, and would have little significance were the most powerful groups in agreement. Of greater interest, therefore, are those restraints which operate upon and help to shape the system as a whole: the political culture and the system of government.

In certain respects the British political tradition is hospitable to pressure-group activities. Both S. H. Beer and H. Eckstein, perceptive American students of British political life, have been struck by its 'persistent corporatism', to use the latter's phrase. Once established as important and 'responsible', groups derive a legitimacy from this tradition such that not to consult them over a relevant item of policy constitutes accepted criticism of a government, and that a measure has been agreed with the relevant organizations is a common recommendation for it. The widespread attitude of deference towards authority, which is well documented in relation to government, seems to extend to other kinds of leadership too, including pressure-group leaders who gain room to manoeuvre from their members which facilitates consultation and, above all, negotiation with the government.[3] There is therefore no general feeling of a necessary conflict between sectional or group interests, and notions of the general or public interest. On the other hand, the government is accorded considerable respect, is expected to govern, and is seen as the principal guardian of the public interest with a duty, among other things, to maintain some kind of balance between different elements in society. There are, of course, different views as to what constitutes a 'balance' or what 'fair play' or 'the public interest' requires—but, in public debate and in Whitehall, for example, the important point is that

---

[1] Thus a doctor who collects stamps would, in the unlikely event of a conflict, probably prefer the BMA to a philatelic society, and, within the BMA, doctors were in fact prepared to withdraw from the National Health Service over a salary dispute in 1965 more readily than they were to stay out of it over certain administrative procedures in 1947. See H. Eckstein, op. cit., and S. E. Finer, op. cit., p. 125.

[2] For an excellent analysis of the conflicting aims, etc., within CND, see F. Parkin, op. cit., and also Ch. 5 below.

[3] See G. Almond and S. Verba, *The Civic Culture* (Princeton University Press, 1965); E. A. Nordlinger, *Working Class Tories* (Macgibbon & Kee, 1967); D. Butler and D. Stokes, *Political Change in Britain* (Macmillan, 1969); and H. Eckstein's emphasis on negotiation, op. cit., Ch. VII.

a group must argue its case in these terms, and, to maximize its impact, provide at least a rationalization of respectability (which will carry conviction in inverse proportion to its lack of substance).

Types of pressure are also affected by prevailing standards, and particularly by the role-definitions applicable to Ministers, MPs, and civil servants. By comparison with the USA perhaps the most conspicuous aspects of this are the absence of any legislation covering the publication of names and expenditures on the part of groups trying to influence legislation, the somewhat less rigorous requirements about the declaration of interests by politicians, and the much sterner attitudes towards, as well as the stricter definition of, corruption.[1]

These factors are important because they help to explain why groups rarely exploit their full potential bargaining power. But it would be naive to think that such things as respect for the conventions of political life and the legitimate government, even when reinforced by the need to maintain group cohesion, come near to being a full explanation of why it is, for example, that more organizations do not adopt disruptive tactics, since attitudes are not immune to experience, and respect needs continuously to be earned. The other essential explanation is that, in its relations with pressure groups, as in all other respects, government is not condemned to a purely passive role. Pressure groups are dependent upon it, and the whole pressure system reflects the behaviour and organization of government as well as its own inner dynamic.

Underlying all relations between government and others is the fact that the government controls resources of the same kind as the groups, and, with respect at least to some of them, will normally be much better placed than any group. A British government, for example, not only has that usual characteristic of modern government, a monopoly of the legitimate use of force and violence, but is widely accepted as legitimate, has extensive control over economic activity, and, through taxation, over some of its proceeds, is reasonably well organized, can rely on widespread communication of its activities (and regulate the conditions under which others may communicate) and has certain advantages over other organisations in any attempt to mobilise general public support. Above all, many of the purposes of others can be furthered only with the support connivance or inactivity of government. This is only to say that in any country which is genuinely *governed*, 'private' groups must share control over resources with government just as in any but a literally totalitarian country, government must share the control of resources, and above all the opportunity to organize, with 'private' groups. But it must always be remembered that, at any given time, many resources will be uncontrolled

---

[1] On the last point, see H. H. Wilson, *Congress: Corruption and Compromise* (Holt, Rinehart, 1951), esp. Chs. 13 and 14. On the lack of publicity in Britain, see S. E. Finer, op. cit., Ch. 9.

or uncommitted (especially the support of large sections of the general public) and that all political resources are ultimately reducible to the behaviour of the people who must sustain both the government and the pressure-group system. Relations between government and groups, even if one attends only to their control of resources, is not literally comparable to a mechanical parallelogram of forces or a set of vectors: the 'forces' concerned in politics are too independent, in their nature and intensity (and not merely in their joint effect), for the comparison to be reliable. Resources are a target as well as a weapon; and usually they are divided, or shared, between the government and others—with control being conditional for both.

The activities of pressure groups are a response to as well as a possible influence upon both the structure of government and the policies of government. At its simplest this means that pressure groups will try to influence government at those points in its structure which are most rewarding in terms of their ability to take the decisions which the group wants taken (which will be a function of the organization of government, the policies of government and the purposes of the particular group). If, however, a group cannot get through to them, it will direct its efforts to the points which are accessible to the group (which will be a function of the organization of government, the resources of the group, and of the group's relationship to the channels of access within the system).

Important features of the British pressure-group system follow from these basic general tendencies. It is now a commonplace to point out that the concentration of power and responsibility in Ministries and their Departments, for all aspects of government, means that pressure groups similarly concentrate their attention on the administration. For the same reason, pressure groups tend to be organized on more centralized and national lines than their counterparts in, say, the United States with its federal system and the adherence to the separation of powers at each level of government. It seems also to be the case that the more centralized and discernible the location of responsibility for the actions of government, the greater the incentive for decision-makers to relate their decisions to the wider and more enduring aspects of their decisions, and thus to resist the narrowest requests of any group, and the greater, too, will be their capacity to mobilize other parts of the governmental machine in their support. This organizational factor clearly reinforces—as it derives reinforcement from—the cultural emphasis upon the 'general interest' we have already mentioned. Conversely, once agreement has been reached, the greater and more assured is the possible 'pay-off' for a pressure group. Similarly, the more 'responsible' is a group's leadership and the more effective their control over their group, the more closely will a government be prepared to involve it in the decision-making process. A pertinent contrast may be drawn here between the role of the major Swedish producer groups in economic planning, especially with respect to prices and incomes, and that of their British equivalents. In Sweden they have both stronger disciplinary powers over their own members and a more decisive part in government. In Britain, to date, the connection between the two phenomena seems to have been perceived more clearly by government than by the groups concerned.[1] On the other hand, to the extent that closer involvement with government, and greater responsibility for decisions taken, implies some 'taming' of the group, and possibly greater difficulty in agreeing on group policy, there are strong tendencies militating against the kind of centralization necessary for the most effective pressure.[2]

The tendency for pressure groups to direct their attention towards the administration does not operate universally. It applies primarily to role-groups, because they alone can readily claim to negotiate on behalf of a determinate clientele which is likely to feel bound by an agreement and because they are more likely to control such resources as security and parts of the economy. Furthermore, by way of contrast, the objectives of a promotional group typically will challenge a policy-premise which can be changed only at a higher or more public level than the kind of issue which constitutes the bulk of government/role group discussion. The parliamentary and public propaganda campaigns therefore tend to be more necessary, and the political party channels of access more appropriate, for promotional groups. No group, of course, can totally neglect them. Producer-groups, for example, may find that the department with which they have most dealings and which is most dependent upon their co-operation is prevented from agreeing by opposition from other, and more independent, parts of the machine; and promotional groups have no monopoly over wider policy matters. But in all cases the ultimate goal must be to persuade Ministers and civil servants, since they alone, as the British constitution now works, have a reliable power of veto as well as the assumed ability to initiate.[3]

At present, it is worth noting, the structure of government seems broadly to satisfy the major established role groups. Complaint emanates principally from some back-bench MPs, academics, and what might be

---

[1] As emerged most clearly from Labour's abortive attempt in 1969 to strengthen the official trades union leadership against 'unofficial' activists, and to push the union movement as a whole into giving power to its central Council and Congress.

[2] The degree of central organization which does obtain in Britain should therefore be seen, perhaps, as a testimony to the potent effect of government structures.

[3] In contrast to, e.g., the US Congress, where the veto-power is widely shared —where, therefore, there are numerous worthwhile points of 'defensive' access and, consequentially, where an immense campaign may be required to carry through a successful initiative.

called the 'pool' of radically-inclined activists from whom many of the reformist promotional groups draw much of their initial support. If, however, such institutions as the advisory committee (which advise *Departments*, not Parliament) did not exist, one would probably find some of the major role, and especially the producer groups, joining in the demands for reform of the committee system of the House of Commons in order to provide both a source of information about government and a more effective route of access to the administration. The existing arrangements, this is to say, tend to favour the major producer groups as against other actual or possible groups.

Government policy is, perhaps, the single most important influence upon pressure groups. This is most obvious in the extent to which the number of organisations involved in the pressure system has increased virtually *pari passu* with the extension of government responsibilities in the social and economic fields.[1]

It is government policy which in large measure determines the need for pressure-group activity. At the same time, as Professor Eckstein has argued, to the extent that a government has a clear policy in a given area (as opposed to simply accepting a responsibility to do something in that area), the scope for influencing government is restricted. The basic reason for this, of course, is that policy provides civil servants and others with guide-lines in their discussions with group spokesmen and that, however important group pressures may have been in helping to secure the adoption of the policy, policy tends to reflect wider constellations of demands and supports than are embodied in the groups most directly affected whose influence, therefore, tends to be confined to relatively detailed issues of application.[2]

The generalizations made in the last paragraph are not, of course, unconditionally valid. Much of what passes for a government's policy in fact emanates from the experience of but one department, experience which will be conditioned by the continuing interaction between that department and its constellation of pressure groups—which is not to say that it will necessarily be urged by those groups.[3] Not all governments are so organized internally for a policy-decision to serve as a meaningful guide-line.[4]

[1] See S. E. Finer, op. cit., pp. 6–8, and the *Report of the Committee on Intermediaries*, Cmd. 7904 of 1950.

[2] On this whole issue, see H, Eckstein's account of the role of the British Medical Association with respect to the National Health Service in *Pressure Group Politics*, op. cit. This general argument is borne out by most other case studies of British pressures.

[3] For a detailed account of a somewhat special case of such interaction, see P. Self and H. Storing, *The State and the Farmer* (Allen & Unwin, 1962).

[4] See, to take but one example, J. S. Martin, *All Honourable Men* (Little, Brown, 1950), for an account of the obstacles in securing adherence to Presiden-

And, above all, they depend on the nature of the political leadership, by which one means principally the nature of the party system: in particular, the extent to which parties are concerned with principle and whether or not they see themselves as 'governing parties'. These factors are the main ones because they directly affect the extent to which parties are capable of distancing themselves from the groups which are most clearly associated with them, the extent to which there are incentives to do so, and the likelihood of their having a distinct perspective or sense of direction when in office.[1] These factors are important, too, in the sense that they influence, in conjunction with the structure of government, the level at which particular decisions are taken and hence the degree of accessibility to what groups.

One may summarize this part of the argument in terms of effectiveness by saying that the influence of any pressure group and the part played by the pressure system as a whole is a function of government policy, the parties, and the structure of government (which interact with one another as well as with outside organizations). In general, pressure groups will be least influential on fundamental issues of policy which are central to the programme of the party (or coherent coalition of parties) in office and when the party is permitted, constitutionally and administratively, to exercise effective guidance over the general conduct of government; furthermore, the arena, within government, in which decisions are shaped or taken will tend to affect, differentially, the pressure-group participants.

In yet more general terms it may be concluded that, in any political system, the world of pressure groups is patterned, the structure being shaped by the resources and channels of access available to the groups, the political culture, and the policies and institutions of government, all of which interact with one another.

---

tial policy by the US Military Government in Germany immediately after World War II. In general this seems to be a greater problem in the American than British system.

[1] This is only to restate the normally accepted arguments about the British and other party systems, and so they do not require elaboration here.

5

Groups in Action

The empirical study of pressure-group activity suffers from two major limitations, one practical and the other theoretical. The practical limitations are the simple difficulty of securing access to documents (and records of telephone conversations) or of having sufficiently detailed discussions with strategically placed participants in the policy-making process. By way of contrast with British experience, the relatively large number of points of access to American governments, at which negative and obstructive pressures, at least, can be brought to bear, tends to bring more of the interaction between organized groups and political actors into the open. Conflicts will frequently be publicized and the arena over which a particular issue is being contested will be enlarged, as groups compete by bargaining and making coalitions. American social scientists who have given their attention to British politics frequently point out the much more secretive, inward-looking, and self-contained nature of pressure politics in Britain. As Beer has argued, this is a consequence of the executive centre of gravity in the functioning of British institutions, the less fragmentary nature of the organization of the major groups in British society and the assumptions that have evolved about legitimate definitions of confidentiality and secrecy.[1] Norman Vig, for example, notes in his study of science and technology in British politics, that though the President of the Royal Society, claimed in his annual Presidential Address in 1964 that the representations made by the Royal Society before the 1962 Trend Committee on the reorganization of civil science had been very influential on government policy, he himself could find out nothing about the detailed proposals, 'which were kept secret even from the Fellows at large'.[2] Whilst this kind of limitation may drive journalists to flights of imagination or intuition, it tends to reduce academics to opaque generalities and the construction of broad typologies that at some points remain respectfully distanced from the facts.

[1] S. H. Beer, *Modern British Politics* (Faber, 1965).
[2] Norman Vig, *Science and Technology in British Politics* (Pergamon Press, 1968), p. 183.

However, there is also the theoretical limitation. Even good case studies will not necessarily produce the kind of generalization and theory we need for a discussion of the major themes which we summarize under the rubrics of representation, rationality and democracy. Each unique and particular case study needs to find a place in a broader theoretical scheme that is attached to the major substantive considerations. Here, as Lowi has argued in a discussion of an outstanding American case study, American productivity in assembling evidence has not been matched by the development of any theory or principles that are sufficiently comprehensive to organize a general discussion of the distribution of power in a society or the successes or limitations of its institutions.[1] A theory would provide something more than a typology that would make the basic Aristotelian distinction between genera and differentiae,[2] or broad classes of pressure group and the broadly similar but still distinguishable sub-categories of which they are composed. It should enable us to formulate in specific terms some other questions; where and in what sense can we identify the elusive quality of rationality in a given pattern or system of representative institutions; what are the implications of these patterns of interaction, in different kinds of group involvement, for the value we wish to identify in political life; what constraints and opportunities do they create for different kinds of pressure for change?

We will approach this level of analysis initially by way of a discussion of a specific political arena, the politics of science, relating it to themes pursued in previous chapters, and then using it as a basis from which to differentiate other kinds of political arena, involving different political actors, different resources, and carrying different implications for the broader themes which we would like to keep within reach of the available evidence.

Government and science
The development of science and technology is a relentlessly accelerated historical process to which national boundaries and political, administrative and social structures seem largely irrelevant. In detail, however, the directions it can take are still subject to choice, within the constraints set by resources and by the institutional structures in which the choices have to be made, as well as the perceptions and beliefs about the role of science that are held by elite groups and by different publics.

The scientific method of the past three centuries, the construction of

[1] T. Lowi, 'American Business, Public Policy, Case Studies and Political Theory', a review article on R. Bauer, I. de S. Pool, and L. Dexter, *American Business and Public Policy: The Politics of Foreign Trade* (Atherton Press, 1963), in *World Politics*, XVI, 1963–4, pp. 677–715.

[2] Aristotle, *Metaphysics*, 1057–9.

theories and the use of mathematical analysis, led gradually to a revolution, or rather a whole series of revolutions, in the natural and physical sciences in the past half-century that have radically altered concepts of reality and have produced an exponential rate of growth in the development and application of new techniques. Nothing, from the preparation for war to the structure of the labour force or decisions about priorities in primary- and secondary-school education, remains untouched by these extraordinary developments. At the start of the Second World War, J. D. Bernal claimed for the social implications of science:

'Science implies a unified and co-ordinated and, above all, conscious control of the whole of social life; it abolishes or provides the possibility of abolishing, the dependence of man on the material world. Henceforth society is subject only to the limitations it imposes on itself. There is no reason to doubt that this possibility will be grasped. The mere knowledge of its existence is enough to drive man on until he has achieved it. The socialized, integrated, scientific world organization is coming. It would be absurd, however, to pretend that it had nearly arrived, or that it will come without the most severe struggles and confusions. We must realize that we are in the middle of one of the major transition periods of human history.'[1]

It is even clearer now, perhaps, than it was then, that the problems of surviving the period of transition are political ones that involve conflict and choice, and that there is nothing in the powerful rationality of the scientific method itself that will resolve them. Whatever the capabilities or potentialities of science may be, the resources it can use, of energy, material and skill, are limited. Complex choices have to be made, some of them to meet remote but threatening possibilities, some of them mortgaging the resources of future generations. The rationality of science itself is only one strand in the historical development. Others are more vulnerable and constantly pulling in different directions.

At one level, where conflicting alternatives present themselves as disputes about the fundamental nature and goals of society, J. D. Bernal himself, with others like Professor Blackett, has been an important participant. It is at this level that science itself, whatever its capacity for determining the best available means to a specific end, can contribute least. The rationality in terms of which we respond to conflicts at this level is concerned with the justification of values, alternative or differing perceptions of the actual and potential nature of a society, of competing claims to be able to provide valid descriptions of the social reality we inhabit. We can distinguish it for our convenience

[1] J. D. Bernal, *The Social Function of Science* (Routledge & Kegan Paul, 1939), p. 409.

from other dimensions by referring to it as substantive rationality.[1]

However, as was pointed out above in connection with the intervention by various groups in the reorganization of the metropolitan structure of London's government, arguments that are concerned with attempts to realize in a specific situation the values that are expressed in deeply internalized attitudes and expectations, will often tend to take the form of disputes about the structures and processes within which decisions about competing priorities will be made, because alterations in the structure of the institutions shift the balance of power and alter the relative chances of survival of different kinds of initiative or different sets of priorities. Depending on the observer's perception, one kind of decision-making process may seem more rational than another. But however difficult to distinguish in empirical reality, it does seem worth making an analytical distinction between a substantive and a processual rationality. A rationalization of the process of decision-making about science has been argued for by people with very different views of what the priorities of national science policy should be. Where demands for resources and specialized manpower become increasingly particular and complex, an institutional system that cannot, for example, inform itself and anticipate demand will not function whatever priorities it is working to, whether they be defence and nuclear energy, as has in fact been the case, or the known and, as Bernal has argued, hitherto unrealized physiological and social needs of the society.

There is, finally, a third dimension to the concept of rationality which we need to distinguish as instrumental rationality. This is, at its simplest, the rationality of a particular technological development, the rationality that is concerned with the best available means to achieve a defined end, whether it be getting a rocket into orbit or preventing a famine. But instrumental rationality is also manifest in political action and as such overlaps with the processual rationality of the institutions. Politicians have, generally, a number of limited and clearly defined ends, such as securing office and avoiding public disfavour, which the political institutions insist on, as it were, as prerequisites for success in the pursuit of grander and more substantive objectives.

The reason, clearly, for making these distinctions between the substantive, the processual and the instrumental components of the concept of rationality is that they help us to locate and identify conflicts that occur in a thoroughly messy reality. For instance, as Downs has argued,[2] the rational politician will sometimes do or say things in the interest of his immediate requirements that reduce the likelihood of a rational con-

---

[1] See the discussion of 'substantial' rationality in D. Kettler, 'Political Science and Political Rationality' in D. Spitz, (ed.), *Political Theory and Political Change* (Atherton Press, 1967), pp. 59–89, and especially pp. 60–7.

[2] A. Downs, *An Economic Theory of Democracy* (Harper & Row, 1957).

sideration of substantive or procedural issues on the part of those he represents, perhaps because he simply fails to formulate a significant issue, or because he is not prepared to share the valuable resource of information. His decision to do so may not of course be entirely self-interested; he might see this exercise of representative discretion as necessary to avoid a popular response that would be irrational in the sense that it would be the outcome of a sudden shift of mere opinion, unattached to any broader awareness of its implications.

We can identify interactions of this kind in a necessarily cursory and superficial survey of Vig's recent account of the irruption of science as a major policy area in British politics.

Unlike many polarizing issues, national science policy is not closely identified with any broad 'interest' in society. There are no historical memories which tend to make voters associate it in some way with partisan differences. Beyond a general consensus that scientific progress is a good thing, there were few clearly defined aspects to it as far as the general public was concerned, until the successful slogan the 'brain drain', simplifying the problem of resource allocation, focused attention on an easily grasped and eminently publicizable consequence of the undernourishment of science in Britain. Furthermore, the really 'attentive public' of the scientists themselves has in fact no clearly identifiable general interest and is consequently difficult to combine behind a broad co-ordinating organization. Demands on resources by scientists typically relate to specific projects in particular fields, and the distribution of resources is not generalized, as it is to pensioners or schoolchildren, but channelled out through many agencies as a result of negotiation between officials and research centres or even individuals. A combination of the fissiparous nature of rapidly evolving technologies and a governmental organization that has grown up in an *ad hoc* way has created an internally competitive pluralism between different fields and their associated agencies, in which there was little incentive for networks of professional groups, dispersed throughout industry and research and educational organizations, to produce a common representative organization. Organizations like the Association of Scientific Workers, in which Bernal and Blackett were prominent, and the British Atomic Scientists Association were intermittently active, though the extent of their influence cannot be assessed. But in general, in Vig's words, 'If scientists were represented in government, it was mainly in their capacity as civil servants, or as individual experts serving on advisory committees. Indeed, as scientists were established in such positions, policy questions largely reverted to government administrators and the traditional processes of informal liaison between such officials and their colleagues in the leading scientific societies.'[1]

[1] Vig, op. cit., p. 27.

However, both the scientists themselves and other publics as well were potentially significant participants in the discussions of national science policy. The extent to which science policy might become a salient issue for them depended first of all on uncontrollable factors, such as the economic squeeze which affected university expansion generally in 1961–2, Russian and American developments and reactions to them, and the skill or luck of opinion leaders or politicians who might be able to formulate issues, whether with ideological or partisan ends in view, in ways that would stimulate anxieties or hopes in politically significant groups. A great deal depended therefore on the quality of the discussion within the elite. And here the significant debate was not between an establishment and groups such as the VIP club of scientists formed to advise Gaitskell and the Labour Party in 1956. (The VIP group were making radical and substantive proposals in several areas, which even the Labour Party leadership at that time was not prepared to consider.) The debate, in which the historically 'reactionary' perspective on the role of science initially held the field, was between Lord Hailsham, not only Minister of Science but Conservative Party philosopher as well, and the radical and technocratic perspective of Aubrey Jones, who had resigned his ministerial post over the reorganization of the Ministry of Supply in 1959; the debate was conducted in intricate processual terms, which had important implications of a substantive nature. Hailsham in effect confirmed, on general philosophical grounds, a *laissez-faire* situation. He thought of science very largely in terms of basic research and consequently saw the issue of government direction and planning in terms of a potential threat to the autonomy of the institutions, mainly the universities, which could protect science from the corrupting influence of commercial or military pressures. According to Vig, this preoccupation affected his awareness of the problems of technological development, and indeed 'he gave little attention to technological development; rather he projected his beliefs about support of pure science into this sphere'.[1]

Aubrey Jones, on the other hand, argued (with initial lack of success) for a much more tightly integrated institutional structure, which would be based on the recognition that far from occurring spontaneously, scientific advances needed the most carefully organised guidance, particularly in the borderlines between disciplines and proliferating techniques. This structure would radiate from an 'industrial and technological nucleus of the Ministry of Science'. He claimed that the competitive free-enterprise system had become irrational for the purposes of modern science, that trade secrets, the absence of links between different companies in related fields, and the complex demands of the profit motive inhibited rather than encouraged adequate research and development

[1] Vig, op. cit., p. 173.

programmes. However, his maverick role as a vocal opposition within his own party isolated him from partisan support, though he had allies in industry. The Conservative Government made some moves towards meeting the kind of criticism he raised, but always under the restraining influence of attitudes articulated for the party by Hailsham.

There were of course many other participants. One such was the Economics Committee of Professor Carter in the Department of Industrial and Scientific Research, which began a series of confidential investigations into a number of industries, starting with the machine-tool industry in 1959. Another was the 1960 Committee, chaired by a Conservative MP, Robert Carr, whose conclusions followed fairly closely behind those of Aubrey Jones, and some of which were supported by the subsequent Trend Committee, appointed in March 1962.

All this discussion between senior advisors and politicians, stimulated more by international comparisons and anxieties about national economic survival than anything that could be described as grass-roots activity, was gradually altering the perceptions of officials and representatives. At the same time, by clarifying the ramifications of science policy it was permitting party leaders to grope towards a party 'policy' in a more public arena, by revealing the opportunities that could be taken to secure partisan credit from the inadequacies of political opponents, to attract the favourable attention of groups other than the scientists themselves on issues related to science policy, and to try to identify the party in a general sense with positive evaluations of the position of Britain in the international exploitation of scientific developments. For example, the university community, together with a more loosely-defined general public, became involved in the process of discussion as a result of the squeeze affecting university places in the early 1960s, though the grounds for their interest was less science policy itself than the shortage of university places. This associated issue mobilized the attitudes towards equal opportunity in education which had also underlain the teachers' concern over the administrative restructuring of Greater London. Subsequently, as the Labour Party's thinking on science policy developed, the National Executive Committee attempted to create clientele groups among academics by involving them in Standing Conference meetings in London and the provinces.[1]

Though it is possible to regard this merely as an instrumentally rational and 'political' attempt to try and improve Labour's image among a group of voters, academics in scientific fields who had hitherto tended to identify their interests with the success of the Conservative Party, it can hardly be denied that this unprecedentedly flexible attempt to nudge an important public into more effective involvement increased the level of information available to the policy-makers. This development, parti-

[1] Vig, op. cit., p. 103.

cularly among the specialist science policy groups of the Labour Party, by providing a basis for opposition to the Trend Committee's proposals for reorganization, which had been developed within the cloistered privacy of the Civil Service, initiated and institutionalised a continuing process of discussion. The Ministry of Technology was one outcome, and the formation of the parliamentary Select Committee on Science and Technology was another. Though short-run partisan forces have been influential, the effect has been to increase the possibilities for the systematic contribution of informed and constructive advice and criticism, within the limits of the broad agreement on priorities which is shared by leaders of both parties. Despite the efforts of the Labour Party in particular, science, as opposed to economic growth, has not become a salient issue for a wide general public, but the potential attentive public is better able to participate, as a result of the debate of the past few years, than it had been.[1]

There are a number of points worth stressing about this particular case before going on to look at others. The first is that although scientists have certain things in common, and in particular a desire that a sufficient proportion of the nation's resources be devoted to science, nevertheless this common concern is not sufficient basis for agreement on policy among the country's scientists. On the contrary, science has operated within a traditional role-definition which stresses the autonomy either of the individual scientist, or, more recently, of the scientific team, which is nourished by the fact that science continues to develop in an increasingly specialized way, scientists tending to work on a large number of different problems, requiring different skills and facilities for their solution, within a variety of institutional settings.

Scientists do however have clear lines of access to Government decision-makers. In part this comes through various professional organizations, among which the most prestigious is the Royal Society. But none of these organizations are representative in the sense of being elected by the whole body of scientists or of being in any sense accountable to them. Partly for this reason, none of these organizations therefore can be seen as entirely fulfilling a spokesman role for British science. Scientists also have numerous informal channels of access to Government through those of their brethren who either are working on behalf

---

[1] In a panel survey conducted in Leeds during and after the 1964 election campaign, 21 per cent endorsed as significant the issue of fast and steady growth of the economy before the campaign, but this had risen to 33 per cent after the campaign. The same issue was eleventh in order of importance before the campaign, but had risen to sixth after. The issue of 'meeting the challenge of automation and the scientific age' was endorsed by about 20 per cent both before and after, and moved only from thirteenth to twelfth place in the ranking. Jay G. Blumler and Denis McQuail, *Television in Politics* (Faber, 1968), Table 10.1, p. 171.

of the Government as researchers or administrators, or have permanent or occasional functions as advisers.

What this means in political terms is that scientists constitute a public, albeit a public with certain organizational nuclei, rather than an organized and fully-fledged pressure group. This condition is maintained, despite the growing need for co-operation among scientists, by the existence of multiple sources of support for scientific effort and for the individual scientist, and a wide choice of work place which extends to other countries as well as this one.

As against this somewhat divided interest, the Government is well placed to take the initiative. For one thing it has access to complete information about the way in which scientific effort is being deployed within the country. This comes about very largely from the fact that so much scientific effort is devoted to activities which are covered by a 'security' blanket. Most obviously this is true of the defence effort, but it also extends to some aspects of the nuclear power programme.

Although scientists are disorganized and disunited in the ways in which we have mentioned, nevertheless they are not and were not without resources. They possess an expertise which the Government needs and they represent, perhaps *par excellence*, an example of the bargaining value of scarce skills. The scarcity of these skills, moreover, has been underlined by an increasing demand for the services of scientists, an increase which calls for no further explanation than the Government's appreciation of the extent to which its policies for defence and economic growth (objectives for which there are intense public pressures) are crucially dependent upon scientific and technological invention and co-operation. At the same time, although there was much talk of the brain drain, it is important to remember that there was no agreement on the extent of the drain, or the reasons for it, but that those reasons quite clearly did not include the existence of an organized threat of withdrawal of labour by a scientific pressure group.

Another striking feature of this case was that the focus of consultation with scientists, and of the work of the Trend Committee, was almost entirely on the problems of instrumental rationality. Excluded from discussion were such important issues of substantive rationality as the extent to which scientific effort ought in fact to be devoted to purposes of defence or to the development of nuclear power. The relations between scientists and Government took place, too, within a context of remarkably little general public pressure or interest in anything other than the fruits of scientific effort. In part this is because of the great abyss of naiveté and ignorance separating the scientists from the general public, an abyss only partially bridged by political leadership. Furthermore, most people, one suspects, have a feeling of awe in the face of science and scientists which precludes any questioning even of those substantive issues on which scientists as such are no more qualified to judge than anyone else.[1] This means that even in peace time the decision-making process on the civil use of science is reminiscent of that described by C. P. Snow in his discussion of science and Government in wartime.[2] He described the system as one of closed 'court' politics, a system in which highly technical decisions were often taken on the basis of informal personal relationships (for all that they were also influenced by wider political considerations) and subjected to totally inadequate discussion and criticism. The extent and degree of participation in decisions of a scientific nature seem, at times, to be in inverse proportion to the literally life-and-death significance of the issues involved.

Trade unions

A marked contrast is provided by the relationships between Government and industrial labour as manifested in respect of the proposed legislation on trade unions introduced, and withdrawn, in 1969. This was of course, and at the time of writing still is, a 'hot' political issue. Much of the relevant information is at least publicly accessible, if not widely shared, and there are strong public attitudes even if only of the kind 'something should be done about it'. In this area the Government is dealing not only with a public and a voting block, but also with a major socio-economic interest which is linked to one of the two main political parties and is spearheaded by organizations of considerable effectiveness and with long histories. In this instance, these organizations, after failing to dissuade the Labour Government from preparing legislation, succeeded (apparently) in forcing it to back down on its most controversial proposals, those dealing with penalties for unofficial strikes and laying down procedures to precede any official union-led strike. Throughout, the discussions were conducted (even the 'private' ones) in conditions of considerable publicity.

One of the first, and most notable features of relations between Government and unions in this case was that the Government was extremely well informed of the likely trade union response to its proposals prior to the formulation of legislation. In general, the trade unions have numerous points of access to the governmental machine, and in this case were in fact consulted at all stages. As an indication of the general position, one might cite the fact that even in 1952 the Trades Union Congress was directly represented on sixty-three governmental

---

[1] The only exceptions to this generalization about the lack of questioning about substantive issues were the activities of CND on the defence side, and certain pressures from the oil and coal industries to cut down the competition from nuclear power.

[2] C. P. Snow, *Science and Government* (Oxford University Press, 1961), especially pp. 53–66.

bodies (ranging from the Economic Planning Board to the Road Safety Committee) and that it, and its constituent unions, also helped to fill numerous other boards and committees in a quasi-representative capacity.[1] The trade-union movement also, of course, has direct and formal access through the House of Commons and the Labour Party, as well as extensive informal access to most levels of governmental decision-making. The question arises, then, as to why the Government appeared to ignore the views of the trade unions and why, having done so, it later had to give way to them on a number of substantial issues.

One, and perhaps the principal, reason for the Government's ignoring the advice given was that it had legitimate grounds for questioning the representative quality of trade union spokesmen. Some of these grounds are concerned with the Constitution and structure of the trade-union movement. For example, the Trades Union Congress Council and Conference, although elected by the trade unions, are elected by trade unions of very different types (craft, industrial, professional and general, etc.). Furthermore, the TUC has a Constitution which gives it little or no power over its members, and thus no power to represent in the sense of being able to commit them. Within the individual trade unions themselves, furthermore, there are wide degrees and kinds of accountability. Some have regularly-elected officers, some elect their officers for life, some insist that their officers take few steps without consulting an executive or other committee, and over the whole range of trade unions there are very wide differences in the nature and extent to which trade-union spokesmen are accountable to their rank-and-file members.

Underlying the constitutional and structural factors there is the question of the nature of the attachment of trade-union members to their own organization. As Goldthorpe has said, 'the understanding of contemporary working class politics is to be found first and foremost in the structure of the workers' group attachments'.[2] The essential point here is that the group life of industrial workers has been such, at least in the past, to breed what Goldthorpe has called a 'natural collectivism'. This is to say that the most meaningful social groups, the work place group, the family group, and neighbourhood group have tended to reinforce one another, to be integrated with one another and furthermore to be unified by experience of the wide-ranging distinction between the workers' 'us', and the 'them' in authority. The attitudes stemming from these group attachments and this group experience are, however, not entirely static. There is, for one thing, an increasing shift (particularly amongst more affluent workers) from a 'solidaristic' collectivism to a

[1] The figures are taken from B. C. Roberts, *Trade Union Government and Administration in Great Britain* (Bell, 1956), pp. 554–5.

[2] J. H. Goldthorpe and others, *The Affluent Worker: Political Attitudes and Behaviour* (Cambridge University Press, 1968), p. 82.

more 'instrumental' collectivism whereby the value of collective action through trade unions and the Labour Party is assessed increasingly in terms of the actual 'pay-off' which collective action gives.[1] But not even solidaristic collectivism ever led to complete unity, any more than the workers' loyalty to their own unions has ever been unconditional.[2] Thus, for example, pickets are normally required during strikes and the membership dues paid remain low in comparison with either North American or Western European practice. (Members' reluctance to pay has had an incidental, and disadvantageous, impact on union effectiveness both industrially and politically. It has in particular prevented unions from paying the salaries to its officers[3] or sustaining the research efforts which American unions regard as essential.) Nor has the underlying group life ever been uniform throughout the country. Inevitably the nature of the attitudes developed vary somewhat with differences in the type of industry, in family connection and tradition, in the degree of skill involved in the job, the extent to which a particular community is isolated, and so on.[4]

The group bases for members' attitudes, including their attitude to their union, are therefore changing. On the other hand, it is far from clear that union organization is changing equally rapidly. On the contrary, there are grounds for thinking that traditional union structures provide another example of V. O. Key's organizational viscosity. Perhaps the most conspicuous example is the continuing reliance on the trade-union branch as the basic organizational unit despite the fact that, the printers' and miners' unions apart, it rarely coincides with the focal point of industrial relations, the work place. The problem, as it affects an increasing number of workers in our contemporary mobile society, has been well depicted by Eric Wigham. He writes that 'a branch of the engineers' or electricians' unions in a dormitory area may include members working in many distant places of work and in many different industries. The members are not drawn together by interest in the common problems of their working life. . . . On the other hand, the members of a union at any particular factory may belong to several different branches, and in addition there may be members of many different unions at the factory.'[5] This distinction is clearly one important factor in pro-

---

[1] See Goldthorpe, op. cit., pp. 73–82.

[2] See for example, the comments of members quoted in R. T. McKenzie and A. Silver, *Angels in Marble* (Heinemann, 1968), pp. 126–33; and cf. the similar findings in E. A. Nordlinger, *The Working Class Tories* (Macgibbon & Kee, 1967) pp. 105–8 and 198–204.

[3] B. C. Roberts, op. cit., p. 464, points out that there were no more than 3,000 paid officials (full-time) in Britain in the mid-1950s.

[4] B. C. Roberts, op. cit., *passim*, and see the discussion in Ch. 3 above.

[5] Eric A. Wigham, *Trade Unions* (Oxford University Press, second edition, 1969), p. 168.

ducing low participation at branch meetings, the increased power and importance of the shop steward, and the apparently widening gap between the perspectives of the leaders and of the rank and file which lies behind so many unofficial strikes.

The Government was well aware of these problems of representation in the unions and, therefore, when faced with unwelcome advice from the union spokesmen it decided to go ahead. The result, however, was not to call the leaders' bluff, but a demonstration that at least the more active trade-union members backed them. At this stage the relationship between Government and unions ceased to be simply a matter of access but came to turn crucially on questions of power and of the resources available to the unions in this disagreement. In fact two types of resource seem to have played an important part. The first resource, if it can be so called, was the fact that the Government required union co-operation in other crucial areas, and not only in this one of trade-union legislation. Particularly this was true in the area of the Government's incomes policy and in this context the basic union resource of the strike was directly relevant. The other was the constitutional place of the trade unions within the Labour Party, including both the National Executive Committee and the Parliamentary Labour Party, and the fact that the trade unions in both centres had considerable support from non-union members. The second of these resources was probably the crucial one, in that most observers agree that the unions would have lost this battle had they not been dealing with a Labour government. What is important, however, is not merely the direct influence of union votes and money, but the extent to which common attitudes and the links between unions and party activists at all levels enable the unions to 'win friends and influence people' amongst other groups who are in a position to sway the party leadership. The unions do not run the Labour Party[1] but their role within it is obviously, under appropriate circumstances, an important long-term resource.[2] In any event, despite wide support expressed in the public opinion polls for the Government's proposed legislation, the unions succeeded in upholding, least for the time being, their historical aim of autonomy with regard to their own internal affairs.

With this experience of fairly successful union pressure may be contrasted the experience of those unions which attempted to persuade the Labour Party to adopt a policy of unilateral nuclear disarmament in

[1] The conclusion reached in Martin Harrison, *Trade Unions and the Labour Party since 1945* (Allen & Unwin, 1960).

[2] Sir Dingle Foot, MP, writing in *The Times*, (October 27, 1969) has claimed that the Government's 'surrender was not to the unions but to Parliament'. In our view, this judgment underestimates the influence of the unions upon Parliament, by which, here, can only be meant the majority Labour Party, and upon the extra-parliamentary organs of the Party. The important point was that *on this issue* Party support constituted one major resource for the unions.

1958–63. In particular, one might cite the case of the Transport and General Workers Union, under Frank Cousins, whose votes played a major part in helping to secure a majority for the unilateralist position at the Scarborough Conference of 1960. However, they were unable to prevent Hugh Gaitskell, backed by a fairly united Parliamentary Labour Party, from successfully fighting and fighting again against their decision. One of the important features of the situation and part of the explanation for this failure is that nuclear disarmament fell within what one might call the 'discretionary' area for trade-union leaders,[1] that is to say an area which was remote from that work-place role of the rank and file which formed the basis of union solidarity. But because this issue fell within the discretionary area of leaders there was less ground for politicians to expect union members to give industrial backing to their leaders' position. In fact this message was underlined by the total failure of the direct action wing of the CND to persuade trade unionists to withdraw their labour from nuclear sites and other jobs which seemed to assist the country's nuclear defence effort.[2]

The general position of trade unions as pressure groups is well illustrated by a statement issued by the TUC just after the Conservative Party won the election of 1951. The statement begins by saying that the trade union would judge each issue 'solely in the light of its industrial and economic implication'. The statement then goes on to say: 'In the future, as in the past, we shall urge on the Government those policies which from our experience we believe to be in the best interests of the country as a whole, and from the same standpoint we shall retain our rights to disagree and publicly oppose the Government where we think it is necessary to do so.' The points worth emphasizing here are the concentration on the 'industrial and economic implication' and the later phrase 'from our experience'. Similar remarks could, of course, be made by most established organizations in Britain, one of the commoner forms of self-denial being an anxiety not to prejudice relations with either major party by taking up too 'political' or 'controversial' a stand on matters of partisan dispute.[3] At the same time, almost the whole case for a government's heeding pressure groups, and for not surrendering its judgment to them, is contained in that phrase 'in our experience'. As they bear upon the role of trade unions, moreover, the two phrases are linked, in that it is experience of the General Strike in 1926, as well as of working within the established pressure-group rules, that has led to the

[1] In this instance, the T. & G.W.U.'s espousal of 'unilateralism' was particularly closely linked with the personal commitment of its General Secretary, Mr Cousins, who had taken office in 1956.

[2] One might contrast the refusal of the dockers to work ships destined to help British intervention against the Soviet Union in 1921.

[3] For some striking examples, see M. J. Barnett, *The Politics of Legislation: The Rent Act 1957* (Weidenfeld & Nicholson, 1969), Ch. 8.

trade-union rejection of industrial action for political (in the sense of partisan) purposes. This commitment, or limitation, certainly lessens the potential effectiveness of trade-union action as a pressure group, however, and it is clear that there are many areas of economic life in which the trade unions carry less weight than industrial legislation.[1]

One final point may be made about unions, as it could also be made about the business interest: neither their strength nor their weaknesses, politically, can adequately be assessed solely by reference to their successes and failures as pure pressure groups. Even in the absence of overt pressure such major interests cannot be totally ignored in policy making on any question which they feel to be significant to them. Conversely, and this is one reason why the unions, having helped to create the Labour Party, were drawn by it into wider political activities, no interests can safely rely upon pressure techniques. It must also become more directly involved in shaping the political context within which pressure groups operate. But, even as pressure groups, trade unions benefit from the intimacy, the opportunities for 'pre-natal' influence, upon a party's or a government's frame of reference, which their interest-derived links with the Labour Party provide.

The Campaign for Nuclear Disarmament

The CND illustrates yet another constellation of political forces. Here, for one thing, we have a promotional group, that is to say a group without a clear constituency in terms either of formal role incumbents or of material interest. Moreover, it was a group which had neither assured channels of access to the Government other than general publicity, nor any significant resources except for certain skills as communicators and a background of an inarticulate disquiet amongst a significant minority of the general public. CND itself enrolled only some of this minority, and Parkin in his excellent study[2] makes it clear that only certain kinds of people were attracted to CND, people definable in terms other than the overt single issue of the British bomb (its testing and its use). Thus, of his sample, Parkin found that 80 per cent were middle class and, it is worth noting, on the whole people who were active in other kinds of association and community effort. In particular CND seemed to appeal to people in socially marginal positions, to those who were left wing, to those who within the professions, the arts, and the churches were generally radical and anti-establishment, and to those who were unsympathetic to the world of business and commerce. CND also attracted a fair number of young people who were not, in many cases, otherwise politically involved but were also generally somewhat rebellious. This

---

[1] Investment policy might be cited as one example.

[2] F. Parkin, *Middle Class Radicalism* (Manchester University Press, 1968), on which most of the information in this section is based.

very selectivity of membership helped to eliminate or to antagonize certain potential allies and it undoubtedly reinforced the unsympathetic attitude of the Conservative Government on the formal and overt issue. The nature of CND membership in fact virtually dictated that it should pin its hopes of effective political action on the Labour Party. And these hopes seemed good once certain Labour MPs, left-wing journalists, and trade unions lent their support to the movement. Unfortunately for CND this support was partly of a purely symbolic kind, in that the purpose of much of it seemed to be simply to use the CND as a further weapon with which to remove the allegedly right-wing Gaitskell from the leadership of the Labour Party.

It is sometimes said that groups like CND perform no representative function, in the sense that no one can be sure for whom the leaders speak or whether they speak accurately on behalf of those for whom they claim to speak. True, unlike role groups, there is a sense in which promotional groups have no constituency independent of their own activities; they create their own constituency. But for that reason it can safely be assumed that simply because they are followed, the leaders are at least representative of those followers. Should the group fail to expand or fail to persuade, then the leadership will remain representative only of its own followers (which may not be insignificant, as the followers may constitute a minority with an important point of view). If, on the other hand, the group succeeds, then quite literally it represents the future. In both cases it makes some sense to talk about the group's representative function, for all that such a group is likely to be relatively short-lived, stemming as it does not from an interest but from a conjunction of various shifting groups, attitudes and perspectives at a point defined by a particular issue at a particular time.

Promotional groups in general tend to flourish in areas which are overlooked by political parties and most of the general public, or in areas which are not considered worth while receiving partisan attention or, as in the case of CND, in areas where the party conflict does not reflect some important disagreement within the community. This of course makes their task extremely difficult because there are very few issues capable of attracting sufficient strength to overcome existing party loyalties or to supplant the parties as political reference groups. To the extent, therefore, that the CND failed a large part of the explanation is that they never attracted the support of the controllers of any sufficiently important resource, or, more accurately, that they lost the one major resource they had once Gaitskell died and was replaced by the apparently more left-wing Mr Wilson. Another part of the explanation is that they lost one of their main unifying issues once the international treaty banning atmospheric tests had been signed. CND thereafter declined into disagreement about new policy and new strategy, few members following the Committee of One Hundred into the strategy of direct obstruction. But CND may not have failed: tests were banned, public interest in defence was increased, at least for a time, and many contemporary political activists were first launched through CND. CND may, as Parkin said, have been a cause without an ideology and hence one particularly suited to middle-class radicals in a period when politics were believed to incorporate the end of ideology. But CND helped to end that period by raising, if only symbolically, new issues of substantive rationality. Such movements are essential to any rational processes of democratic government.

Commercial Television

A final example of pressure-group action may be found in the very successful campaign of the Commercial Television lobby. This lobby centred upon a relatively small number of Conservative back bench MPs who, between 1950 and 1955, persuaded their own party to introduce Commercial TV. As H. H. Wilson's account of the campaign shows,[1] the group had certain advantages, of which perhaps the main one was very ready access to their own party in the House of Commons through membership of its broadcasting committee, to the Conservative Party Central Office through some of its officials, and, mainly through Lord Woolton, to the Cabinet. The group also had the advantage of close links with men in the radio and public-relations industries which were productive not only of technical help, but also, on occasion, of finance. Their great achievement lay in successfully overcoming the intense opposition within their own party. The fact is that initially many, perhaps most, Conservative MPs, and certainly most members of the Cabinet, were opposed to Commercial TV; largely this seemed to derive from a feeling that the brashness and vulgarity associated with Commercial Television in America conflicted with the traditional Conservative ideal of public service, an ideal associated in their eyes with the BBC. The group succeeded, so far as one can see, essentially by appealing to the fear that the BBC might be used in peace-time, as it was in war, as a propaganda instrument, and especially that it might be (or even had been) used in a partisan way by a Socialist government. It appealed also to the burgeoning and more militant ideology of private enterprise which was then entering the thinking of the Conservative Party, and to the vision of Commercial TV as a vehicle for inducing the general public to adopt a consumer orientation rather than that identification with their producer roles which seemed to lie at the basis of the Labour Party's appeal. Some members of the Cabinet and their own party seem also to have been persuaded by reference to 'public demand', despite the fact that much of that public demand was artificially produced by the group

[1] H. H. Wilson, *Pressure Group: The Campaign for Commercial Television* (Secker & Warburg, 1961).

itself. Above all, however, the group succeeded because it included dedicated and well-placed men in its ranks, because it gained further support in key places, and because it skilfully exploited the opportunities provided by a widespread desire for change, but a desire unconnected with any precise alternative means of satisfying it. Finally their success may be attributed to the fact that the issue concerned was, or seemed to be, somewhat peripheral to the major issues of politics and particularly of party conflict. There is little or nothing in this story to suggest that a similar group could as easily overcome resistance in its own party on matters of more major and fundamental significance.

Pressure groups and the political process

We may now offer certain general and concluding comments on pressure groups in the light of our discussion in this and the previous chapter. First of all, it is clear that on occasion the sole, or more probably the principal, source of outside critical examination of government behaviour will be one or more pressure groups. Pressure groups can thus contribute to the process discussion. They may also enhance the rationality of decision making, partly because of the information they provide, and partly also simply by making the government offer justifications, and hence perhaps prepare its policy more adequately in the face of different sets of arguments and of new perspective.

Pressure groups may thus also help to round out and complement the formal system of representation. As such they have certain distinctive qualities to offer, and in particular the fact that they can choose the issue and the timing of their own intervention to a greater extent than can the electorate, although even pressure groups must operate within the limits set by government policies and procedures. They may therefore perform an important, vital, and indeed irreplaceable task in lending meaning and specific content to the right of opposition. But it does not follow from this that pressure groups necessarily provide a more rational or more meaningful process of representation than that provided by the parties and electoral system. For this there are three main reasons. Firstly, neither the leaders nor members of pressure groups, for all that they may be drawn from the relatively more concerned and informed, can escape from the limits of their own experience or from the perspectives and attitudes fostered by their own somewhat limited patterns of interaction. Secondly, and this is important from the point of view of what we have called the populist dimension to democracy, there is no pressure group equivalent to universal and equal suffrage. As we have seen, pressure group 'votes' are weighted. Moreover, the incumbents of some roles are much more difficult to organize than are others, consumers being the most obvious example, and the incumbents of many roles or the sharers of many attitudes may lack sufficient agreement on alternative policies to intervene effectively. Thirdly, it is sometimes forgotten, in discussions of pressure groups as contributors to the representative process, that much of the activity of pressure groups and particularly of promotional groups would be virtually impossible but for the channels of access through the party machinery and for an enfranchised general public capable of significant intervention. It follows, too, that in different political arenas not only will decisions be taken at different levels within the Government, but they will also involve different kinds of groups with different channels of access and different resources. This means that on different issues, the same pressure group may be involved in different ways and with different results and purposes. This in turn means that it is very important not to assume that the impact of any particular group or set of groups can be generalized from one case study to another.

It may be suggested, finally, that while pressure groups are necessary to democracy and to an open system of politics, they are far from sufficient. The pressure group system may fail, in fact, to articulate all the relevant interests and perspectives, or to do so in the form or at the time necessary for them to carry any weight. Moreover, it depends upon the constitution and the general political context whether pressure groups operate as a force for enlarging the circles of informed involvement or whether they contribute rather to the creation and maintenance of an exclusive inner circle for confidential bargaining and discussion. We will return to some of these issues in the concluding chapter.

6

Representative Government: Vulnerability and Rationality

Political information: collection and use.

The normal condition of the politician is one of uncertainty, about the nature and strength of the claims on his representative role, about the impact of his own and his colleagues' behaviour on different publics. The mass electorate provides veiled and indeterminate cues and responses, whilst pressure groups provide specific but selective information and lay claims to a representative status that is always open to question. But the politician cannot resolve his uncertainties at a leisurely academic pace. The legislative process runs to an intricate series of deadlines, whilst tactical and strategic success depends on both accurate perceptions and shrewd timing. The politician's general orientation, fostered by interaction with his supporters and colleagues, provides him with a framework by means of which he can place fresh or inherently ambiguous information into a meaningful context. In some respects this social reality will be very widely shared in the society, a consensus on broad features of the political culture. But he will also constantly be interpreting events in ways that are meaningful only within the framework of a particular partisan or ideological framework.

But whatever his ideological or partisan confidence, he is in constant need of digestible information, in the first instance to increase his control over his own options and prospective survival and success, and in the second to perform his role as a representative, exercising his better judgment on behalf of others. It may be difficult to satisfy either requirement; information about the needs and feelings of different publics may be unreliable or too complex to be of direct and immediate relevance. On the other hand, the politician may be able to satisfy the first requirement without being impelled to realize the second. He may avoid information that is in principle available because some kind of decision is required and he can afford to relegate the issue in order to spend more time and attention on more pressing problems. Similarly conflicting calculations apply to his attempts to influence a wider public by publicizing information or starting a debate. He may avoid doing so in order to avoid mobilizing or antagonizing the wrong group, from the instrumental point of view of his personal or partisan objectives, with the result that public discussion might be entirely inadequate to the implications of the policy decisions that are taken.

The flow of political information is in the nature of things uneven and sluggish. Many of the reasons for this have already been discussed. For most people most of the time, political issues are remote and responses to them are shaped in complex and indirect ways by reference groups and the mass media. But the institutional structure within which politicians and opinion leaders operate can serve either to reduce the flow of information and the level of involvement or, to some extent at least, to stimulate it. At best our institutions are an imperfect approximation to the goal of political representation, necessarily so because political representation sets complex demands for a complex and rapidly changing society. Our final concern here is to emphasize the vulnerability of these institutions in terms of the quality of the information available to politicians and administrators and the incentives and constraints that determine its use.

In principle, academic and practical interests converge in the study of the flow of political communication. Such 'academic' concerns as the analysis of electoral behaviour, the impact of the mass media and of the personality or 'image' of political leaders, and the salience of different issues to different groups in the electorate, are also of immediate importance to the parties, which in fact commission surveys with increasing frequency from commercial market research firms.[1] Similar evidence in specific areas is no less important to civil servants who are involved in formulating and implementing policy. But there are serious hindrances to the fullest practical exploitation of such evidence.

Where the practical demands of policy-makers call for valid and broadly useful generalizations at short notice, the better surveys take time to prepare, conduct and analyse, and their more interesting conclusions will frequently consist of qualifications and elaborations, or of the discovery of new and theoretically interesting questions about the nature of the political process. They contribute to our understanding of the themes we have been pursuing, but less obviously or directly to political decisions. The impatience of the active politician is understandable, but unfortunately it is not always accompanied by alternative insights, derived from practical experience, that square with the best empirical evidence we have.[2]

[1] Research Services Ltd are regularly employed by the Labour Party and Opinion Research Centre by the Conservative Party.

[2] See, for example, the skilful but absurdly unfair review of D. Butler and D. Stokes, *Political Change in Britain*, by Iain Macleod, MP, entitled 'The private world of political science', *The Times*, October 30, 1969.

Furthermore, as we suggested in chapter 2 the best survey is still a relatively crude device for extracting patterns of influence and inter-action from the overlapping confusions of reality. In normal circum-stances it is seldom possible to conduct experimental analyses of, for example, the impact of different kinds of communication on attitudes. There is a rapidly growing literature in this field, based on laboratory experiments, but the circumstances, the participants and the nature of the experimental communications cannot bear directly on the kind of question either politician or political scientist is concerned with. On the other hand, the laboratory experiments certainly underline the complexity of the process of communication and the number of factors which have to be taken into account. These include not only the attitude of the recipient to the source or sender, the importance of the message to him, the group pressures he is under, his general predispositions, but also, and evidently in complex ways, the form and order in which conflicting information is presented. Even the survey and the *ex post facto* experimental design can only come to terms with this complexity in approximate ways.[1]

Some general conclusions do nevertheless emerge from recent studies of the flow of communication from politicians and opinion leaders to the electorate. They substantiate the kind of analysis presented here, by stressing the importance of the *structure* of the individual's attitudes and opinions to his responses to fresh information. For example, Blumler and McQuail have isolated the less interested electors in 1964 as most vulnerable to the impact of Liberal Party appeals. Whilst the more interested voters deliberately exposed themselves to election television, sometimes to guide their votes, sometimes to collect infor-mation on their party's position or even just to catch up on what was going on in national politics, the less interested, exposing themselves to partisan messages more or less at random, vaguely dissatisfied and mistrustful of the dominant forces in British politics, could attach them-selves for the occasion to the third party without any psychological discomfort.[2] There are melancholy lessons in findings like these for the managers and theoreticians of minor parties. It is clear, for example, that a substantial proportion of the recent support for nationalist parties

[1] There is an excellent survey of the experimental literature, together with a brief discussion of the broader implications of these studies, in Arthur Cohen, *Attitude Change and Social Influence* (Basic Books, 1964).

[2] Blumler and McQuail, *Television in Politics* (Faber, 1968), Ch. 11. It is also interesting that the source most strongly associated with this response to the Liberals was the television news bulletin, rather than more explicitly persuasive programmes, or radio and the press. The flow of information is substantially affected by attitudes towards the vehicle of the communication. For further evidence, see Butler and Stokes, op. cit., Ch. 10, 'The Flow of Political Infor-mation'.

in Scotland and Wales is of this kind, unstable transfers of support on grounds that may only distantly echo the formulated appeals of minor party leaders. Other support, of course, may be more substantial, particularly from younger voters who have not yet crystallized their party affiliations in an atmosphere which happens in any case to be characterized by increasing volatility of party identification.

Differentiated findings of this kind may assist the parties in tailoring their approaches to different groups of target voters. However, attempts to use surveys to increase the level of information available to policy-makers and politicians about the distribution of attitudes and opinions on particular, but broad, issues raise serious difficulties and there seem to be grounds for anxiety about the relationship between academic and practical demands for information on the currents of public opinion. One risk has already been emphasized, the misreading of fluctuations of opinion with a weak informational base as significant orientations that call for responsive rather than responsible reactions from elected representatives.[1] Another risk, which is suggested by criticisms of a survey commissioned for an important recent publication by the Institute of Race Relations,[2] is that of faulty methodology at a more advanced level. The example happens to arise in an issue area of the greatest importance, where participants in the discussion are very ready to deploy 'facts' and 'information' to support their arguments.[3]

The survey was planned by five distinguished social scientists, including Dr Mark Abrams whose organization, Research Services Ltd, carried out the investigation. The most widely publicized finding relates to the distribution of the sample along what is referred to as a 'prejudice-tolerance scale'. On the basis of scores given to responses to a number of questions (which were unevenly weighted, for reasons that have not been made clear), the sample was divided into four categories, the Prejudiced, 10 per cent, the Prejudice-inclined, 17 per cent, the Tolerant-inclined, 38 per cent, and the Tolerant, 35 per cent. The cut off point between the categories, as Dr Abrams has emphasized, must in the end be an arbitrary decision. However, it is immediately clear that a distribution of this kind would look encouraging to anyone concerned with harmony between the races. The major criticisms that have been

[1] See the useful conceptual distinctions made by Roland Pennock, 'Responsiveness, Responsibility and Majority Rule', *The American Political Science Review*, Vol. XLVI, No. 3, September 1952, pp. 790–807.

[2] E. J. B. Rose and others, *Colour and Citizenship: A Report on British Race Relations* (Oxford University Press, 1969), Ch. 28, 'Attitudes of the British Public'.

[3] See the House of Commons speech by Mr Enoch Powell, MP, on November 11, 1969, reported in *The Times*, November 12, 1969, p. 6, wherein he made considerable and disputed use of Government statistics.

made refer to the construction of this scale and the method of scoring responses to the questions.[1]

A valid and reliable questionnaire scale depends, first of all, on satisfactory conceptualisation of the dimension to be tapped, and, secondly, on the careful selection and testing of propositions that will elicit responses along this dimension. In this study, the conceptualization of the dimension of prejudice-tolerance seems, from the published material, to be partial and far from unambiguous. The scale itself was never prepared or tested. It was in fact constructed after the collection of the data, from the distribution of responses to some fourteen questions. Four of these were selected as particularly important and have been heavily weighted in the scoring. Responses to the others were allowed less significance in the final total. Three of the four key questions refer to housing; none refer to employment or immigration. The critics have argued that the distribution resulting from this procedure is exceedingly misleading, that the reaction of the Prejudiced 10 per cent would better be described as one of 'extreme hostility', and that this puts a very different complexion on the inferences policy makers should draw from the rest of the distribution. As it stands, the incidence of politically and socially significant prejudice is seriously underestimated. Lawrence has also pointed out that by rescoring the responses obtained in the Nottingham area, in a manner that is neither more nor less arbitrary than that actually employed, a radically different picture can be presented.

The survey also employs a crude personality measure of authoritarianism and 'social potency', derived from two questions. We are told that one-fifth of the sample qualified as consistently authoritarian and that these were substantially more colour-prejudiced than were the non-authoritarian. But it would be naive to argue from evidence as cursory as this that there is a causal relationship between the two. It seems more likely that in each case the questions used were really probing into the same general psychological area and that these measures are in fact blunt and undiscriminating.

The remainder of this substantial volume contains important and interesting material, including a case study of the legislative process between 1965 and 1967, but the findings of the survey seem to have achieved a generally uncritical acceptance in the current discussion.

Problems of this kind, particularly where they are obscured by protective technicalities, are worth illustrating at length, because there is a growing sensitivity to the value of the social survey among administrators and politicians. This is in part a reflection of the growing sophistication of survey techniques, but in part also a result of the increasing demand

---

[1] The correspondence appears in *New Society*, 1969: 14 August (John Rowan), 21 August (Daniel Lawrence), 28 August (Mark Abrams), 11 September (Daniel Lawrence).

for data of all kinds as the complexity and scope of governmental involvement in economic and social planning increases, and as the ability to handle such data is increasingly recognized as a necessary accomplishment by politicians themselves. None the less, an attempt to establish and make systematic use of this channel of communication, between publics and policy-makers, followed slowly, as it did in the United States, on the availability of the necessary techniques. In both countries the war precipitated governmental involvement in social management on a large scale. The politician's sixth sense for public opinion needed the support of well-qualified auxiliaries, and in the early 1940s the Government Social Survey was set up as an independent research unit to conduct investigations for the Government Departments. Even after its establishment, the new unit, under Louis Moss who is still its Director, had to live with suspicions about the political risks of probing too sharply into latent and unarticulated currents of opinion as well as about the propriety of such inquiries into the attitudes and behaviour of private individuals. Indeed, the appointment of Mr Boyd-Carpenter as Financial Secretary to the Treasury in 1951 led to the suspension of further survey work with a social-psychological orientation, and a temporary shift to the collecting of statistics.[1] But more recently the unit has come to occupy an established position as a source of specific information on public attitudes and behaviour, with its own fund of expertise and experience on every phase of the exacting task of securing valid information from representative samples.[2] The discussion of policy on something as highly political and generally salient as taxation can now make use of the standing Family Expenditure Survey to maintain a continuing mathematical model that relates the spending patterns of different groups to changing taxation policies. In this area, and in many others, Government Departments actively search for information to feed into complex decision-making processes. It may be more reliable and is likely to be more comprehensive than information brought to their attention by organized interests, and may bear on the lives of people who are, in some respects, poorly represented or not represented at all by any organization with access to decision-makers.

The availability of survey techniques and the existence of organiza-

[1] See the Appendix to P. G. Gray and T. Corlett, 'Sampling for the Social Survey', *Journal of the Royal Statistical Society*, Series A (General), Vol. CXIII, Part II, 1950. This contains a selection, with summary descriptions, of a number of surveys conducted between 1946 and 1949. See also *Government Social Survey. List of Published Reports and Papers* (HMSO, serial). The subjects range from 'Public Opinion and Colonial Affairs' (119, 1948) to 'Scientific Manpower' (190, 1952) and 'Adolescents in Britain' (148P, 1950).

[2] The Survey publishes important methodological papers, for example Christopher Scott, 'Research on Mail Surveys', GSS m.100; Jean Atkinson, *Handbook for Interviewers*, GSS M.136; Gray and Corlett, op. cit., GSS M.58.

tions, such as the Government Social Survey and some of the commercial polling organizations, are potentially valuable additions to the network of political communication. They can throw light on obscure and complex situations and contribute to a rational analysis of alternatives by Parliamentary committees, Ministers, and civil servants. However, they are only auxiliary sources of information. They suffer from their own inherent limitations, liability to error and crudity. And their mere existence does not protect the democratic process from its own vulnerabilities. Information can be misperceived by politicians no less than by voters. In fact, as we have seen, the coherent and integrated perspectives on political affairs that are developed by those who are most intensely involved can, on occasion, trap them within the bounds of their own limited perceptions and aspirations. There are many ways in which fresh or challenging information can be interpreted to fit preconceptions or brought into line with the received social reality of a group.[1]

Above all, fresh information can simply be avoided, a substantial temptation when decisions have to be given complex legal formulation against the pressure of time. Administrative and political structures may, as we saw in the discussion of science policy, restrict the flow of necessary information, but even where the information is in principle available there may be many reasons why it is ignored. The Ministry of Housing and Local Government, for example, made no reference whatsoever to the Government Social Survey between 1951 and 1957, despite the fact that it sponsored Acts of Parliament in 1954 and 1957 dealing with the socially sensitive problem of privately rented housing. One result of this has been summarized by the author of an invaluable and comprehensive study of the Rent Act of 1957, where he points out that 'the regulators, be they Government or Parliament, knew remarkably little about what they proposed to regulate. Nor did this seem to be of great concern to the participants. Neither Government front or back bench, nor the Opposition, seemed much concerned about the extent of their own ignorance.'[2] But it is not only in this respect that the history of that Act is relevant to our argument. The explanations Barnett suggests for its failures touch on most of the themes with which this book has been concerned, and together highlight the precariousness of the discussion and representational process in the UK. It is therefore worth looking at this final case as evidence, not of the typical manner of proceeding of British Government (at least one trusts that it is not), but rather of the points at which

[1] See D. McQuail, *Towards a Sociology of Mass Communications* (Collins-Macmillan, 1959) and Cohen, op. cit., especially Ch. 7, 'The Influence of the Group, and Ch. 8, 'Attitudinal Inoculation and Immunisation'.

[2] Malcolm Joel Barnett, *The Politics of Legislation: The Rent Act 1957* (Weidenfeld & Nicholson, 1969), p. 261. We have drawn heavily upon this fascinating and illuminating case-history in the ensuing discussion.

and the ways in which even firmly established political structures and processes may fail to achieve their ends.

A legislative failure

The main provisions of the 1957 Act lowered the ceiling on the value of private rented accommodation the rents of which were controlled, increased the permissible rents in those properties which continued to be controlled, provided for the de-control of all property on a change of tenancy, and made it slightly more difficult for tenants to prevent rent increases by obtaining certificates of disrepair. The stated intentions of the legislation were to increase the return to the landlords and to move towards a free market in housing. These aims were pursued in the belief that they would produce a more rational use of existing property by encouraging mobility, provide new incentives to carry out repairs, and induce investors to increase the stock of new rented accommodation. In no respect did the Act have precisely the intended results.[1]

The Act failed mainly because of a faulty appraisal of the number of houses affected, of the potential or actual demand, and of the relevant factors determining present and future supply and because of a misreading of the lessons of interwar legislation. For this faulty appraisal the primary explanation seems to be that the Executive, at both the Ministerial and civil service levels, failed to seek out or use the information necessary to combat the weight of precedent, party doctrine, and conventional wisdom. This failure is partly explicable by reference to the accidents of personality. The Ministry of Housing and Local Government had lost two of the civil servants who were most expert in the field of rent control. One of them, incidentally left the Department in order to become Secretary of the National Association of Property Owners, which, in the event, turned out to be the most influential (possibly the only influential) pressure group. There was also a new Permanent Secretary whose previous interests had lain outside the field of Rent Control, while much must be laid at the door of the personalities of the two Ministers concerned, Mr Duncan Sandys, and, in the more junior position, Mr Enoch Powell.[2] Another part of the explanation is organizational. The possibility of exposure to unsolicited data was restricted by the practice of confidentiality, which is still the prevailing style of Government Departments, and by due observance of those constitutional proprieties which are designed to safeguard Ministerial power and preserve

[1] See Barnett, op. cit., Ch. 13.

[2] Barnett, op. cit., writes: 'The master of anything he touched, Mr Powell knew what he wanted to such an extent that advice became almost irrelevant' (p. 62), and, 'Apparently Mr Sandys either did not require all the data available or . . . could not absorb all that was presented. In any case, the amount omitted or ignored seemed considerable' (p. 63).

civil-service anonymity. Significantly, few changes were made in the Bill after it was first published and, with the exception of the one pressure group already mentioned, there is no evidence of any substantial influence on policy (as opposed to the 'technical' details) from any source outside the Ministry of Housing and Local Government itself. In other words, Barnett's detailed account suggests that, outside the tiny circle of initiators, nothing occurred which could be dignified by the label of genuine discussion.[1]

This particular piece of legislation does not seem, in retrospect at least, to provide an example of instrumentally rational policy-making. On the other hand, it is difficult, even in retrospect, to condemn the various actors, all of whom can be seen, given their own goals, to have in some sense behaved in an instrumentally rational fashion.

The Cabinet, it is true, seems to have given little consideration to the Bill. But it must be remembered that the crucial policy and drafting decisions were taken in the summer and autumn of 1956, the period of the Suez crisis and, later, of the Soviet invasion of Hungary. It was hardly irrational, under those circumstances, for senior ministers (the pace-makers in any cabinet) to be preoccupied with foreign affairs. Nor was it obviously irrational for Mr Sandys and Mr Powell to feel that housing was an area to which their belief in the virtues of the free market and of private enterprise was particularly relevant. No one, for example, even if it be granted that the 1957 Act was a failure, could make a much more favourable judgment on previous legislation. The civil service is not entirely to be blamed for adhering to a method of incrementalism in formulating the legislation, that is to say, for taking previous legislation as their starting point and incorporating in the new legislation only those devices which had been 'legitimated' by previous use. They cannot be blamed either for feeling that it was perhaps more important to make some decision, and thus end uncertainty, than to undertake extensive new programmes of research as a preliminary to legislation. To have behaved otherwise would have been to expose officials to the familiar charge of dragging their heels by reference to the principle of unripe time. Moreover, the Civil Service would have laid itself open to legitimate criticism if it had disregarded the policy preferences of its Ministerial bosses.

The political parties do not come out of the picture particularly well either; but one can hardly say that it is entirely irrational, given their basic presuppositions, for the Conservatives to have preferred to leave

---

[1] It has been privately suggested to one of the present authors that the circle of initiators was exceptionally small because a number of civil servants, who might normally have been expected to participate, did not in fact play any part; they preferred to stay clear of a Bill which they believed would be inadequate but upon which they felt they could have no effective influence.

this legislation largely to the initiative of their leaders. It must be granted that the Labour Party's opposition, in and out of Parliament, was not very effective and its arguments rarely met those adduced by the Government. Nevertheless, it is possible to maintain that the irrational course would have been to devote its energy to a serious attempt to amend and improve an Act whose premises were fundamentally incompatible with Labour's own policy of transferring private rented accommodation to municipal ownership.[1] Nor was it irrational for certain pressure groups to refrain from bringing their full strength to bear for fear that to interfere in such a controversial issue was to run the risk of becoming unduly involved in party politics. The same may be said about the calculation of other pressure groups that it would be unwise to exhaust their 'credit' with the Ministry of Housing and Local Government by trying to thwart or seriously to modify such a highly charged item of political legislation.[2] From the point of view of those opposed to the legislation, it was certainly unfortunate that the trade-union movement mobilized its resources, such as they were, too late to have any real chance of affecting the situation. The trade Unions were, after all, the strongest established organization to include any significant number of private tenants amongst its members—even if the unions overestimated that number. But, before asserting that their tardy involvement was irrational, it is worth remembering that this was a matter which, by tradition, the trade unions have left to the political wing of the Labour movement and that the latter had espoused a policy about which most trade unionists were neither knowledgeable nor enthusiastic.

Finally, it may be said that the lack of tenant action, of any mobilized consumer opinion, in this area was at least understandable and, indeed, was at least partly to be accounted for by the Government's apparently deliberate failure to publicize its intentions. The Government seems to have felt that rent control was a dangerous issue and likely to spark off highly generalized and doctrinaire responses. They therefore calculated, apparently, that their policy of de-control would have a better chance of acceptance if, so far as possible, popular judgment were deferred until its supposedly beneficial effects were experienced. This calculation can be faulted, of course, on the grounds that the lack of publicity maintained the prevalent public disinterest in the subject (in November 1956 only 7 per cent of a polled sample saw housing as an urgent family problem)[3] and hence cut off one possible source of the information without which

---

[1] The rationality of this solution is not the issue here; it ceased to be Labour policy in 1961.

[2] For an analysis of the same general themes in the setting of County politics, in Cheshire, see J. M. Lee, *Social Leaders and Public Persons* (Oxford University Press, 1963), especially Ch. 6, 'Persons in Public Life'.

[3] Gallup Poll figures cited in Barnett, op. cit., p. 115.

the irrationality of the argument was concealed. Be that as it may, the facts are that the Government provided a minimum of information, that in consequence the press had little to contribute, and that 'the general public were ill-informed, misinformed, and unaware of a "great debate" which might affect the lives of many'.[1] This final point is also germane to any suggestion that public inactivity is evidence of popular irrationality. The point is that under the British political system it is normally assumed that others, more in the know and more expert, will ensure that it is at least plausible to expect the general public to be well informed. That was not so in this particular case.

As we suggested earlier, the experience of the Rent Act is not necessarily typical, nor must one exaggerate the shortcomings of the legislative process which it revealed. It was, or appeared to be, a piece of highly technical legislation, its significance was deliberately played down, and there seemed to exist no informed special public to spell out its implications to the general public. Throughout its history, moreover, the new Act was overshadowed by greater issues. Not only was it introduced against a background of the Suez and Hungary crises, but its Parliamentary debate was affected by a change of Prime Minister and, consequentially, of Minister. None of these conditions are universal in terms of time and issue. It should also be remembered that some important concessions were in fact made about the payment of premiums, the length of the period of transition before de-control, and about the length of notice which tenants must receive on being asked to quit by a landlord. Nor were policy-makers free of certain general political constraints which were, so to speak, built into their own thinking. For example, there was never any serious question of the Ministry's introducing an immediate and totally free market. Nevertheless, the fact remains that the Rent Act of 1957 presents a somewhat feeble illustration of representative government in action.

Too much must not be made of this one case, but, taken in conjunction with our general discussion, it prompts a number of general observations. The first and perhaps the most important is this: we have suggested that by certain tests at least the various actors (and non-actors) could be said to have behaved rationally, although the legislative outcome was far from satisfactory. From this, it follows that what we have called processual rationality is not a simple construct of instrumental pieces of Lego or Meccano. It is at least conceivable, therefore, that a rational process might be built out of individual actions, many of which are highly irrational and, conversely, as seems to have been the case here, that a process of legislation may fall short of an ideal level of rationality even if the individual participants acted in instrumentally rational ways.

In particular, secondly, it is arguable that the prevailing constitu-

[1] ibid., p. 118.

tional procedures associated with the doctrines of Ministerial responsibility no longer amount to the most rational available process. Thus Barnett suggests[1] that civil service concern with its own anonymity and the need to avoid landing Ministers in trouble now results, not in the injection of expertise into the purely partisan, but in curtailing both the contribution of the official expert and the exposure of administration to popular scrutiny.

A third general conclusion is that even in a system many of whose structures and processes can rightly be claimed to be democratic in intent, there is no automatic thrust towards greater involvement in decision making. There is, to put it another way, no automatic processes which ensure that the arena of conflict on important issues is enlarged to include all those, even, who will be directly affected by the decision taken. If the British system of government is to encourage (or even permit) more active and informed involvement in decision taking, there are a number of points at which the history of the 1957 Rent Act shows there to be room for improvement. The House of Commons must be armed with more effective means for the extraction of information and for scrutinising the work of the Executive; there must be much greater publicity and openness in Government processes; by these and other means there must be created some source of viable alternative policies which may reasonably be set beside Government proposals to serve as a basis not only for criticism but for intelligent choice; and, finally, if pressure groups are to make their most constructive continuing contribution to government, namely the supply of information and the communication of experience, then the Government must be so organized as to seek and process relevant data.

It is worth observing, fourthly, that the terms of Bryce's curious interaction between Government and public opinion were, in this context, heavily loaded in favour of the Government. The limits upon its freedom to manoeuvre directly imposed by the general public were wide and ill defined. For this situation, as we have seen, the Government itself was partly responsible, as were the other organizations and institutions, one of whose normal functions is to communicate with the public. But no government could obtain such leeway were it not for the nature of public attitudes and opinions, which we have tried to explore in previous chapters, the diversion of inherently limited political attention to more dramatic events, and the lack of any particular public to perform its surrogate and mediating roles in relation to the public at large.

In this last respect, rented housing is reminiscent of civil science and of nuclear weapons before CND—it was an area in which issues were defined and policies elaborated at the centre and in something approaching a political vacuum. The costs of information, time, and effort are too

[1] ibid., Ch. 1, especially pp. 4–7.

great for it to be reasonable to rely on continuous general public interest in all aspects of government, however important their results.[1] If, in addition, there is no small body of interested and informed outsiders, the result is, as Barnett puts it with reference to the 1957 Act, that:

'Decisions were taken too fast and too unpredictably to permit *ad hoc* research, hence quality of thought and aptness of response depended upon past research and public discussion. If the apparatus of relevant concepts and an educated public opinion, for at least the sophisticated and knowledgeable journalists and politicians was not available, trouble was inevitable.'[2]

Generalizing this observation, we suggest that the bridges between a decision-making elite and the general public must include a comprehensive range of special publics. The opportunity must exist for members of such a public to organize themselves if, on occasion, they are to maximize their impact. But their importance does not lie in a shared interest, outlook, or role of the kind necessary for effective organization; it lies, rather, in their contribution to the discussion process. In any event, the history of the Rent Act underlines the point made in earlier chapters, that, from the point of view of discussion as from that of representation, the world of organization and pressure is an insufficient guarantor of processual rationality.[3] There must also exist others who sustain a close and informed interest in any particular area, who have access to information, and who are in a position to communicate their findings and views to the public at large. To the extent that one is concerned with democratic politics it is also insufficient to focus attention exclusively on special publics. It is probably true that their existence and multiplication is dependent upon the existence of a wide general public with meaningful political rights. But their justification lies not only in their contribution to rational decision making through critical and open discussion, it lies also in their role as actual or potential catalysts of general public involvement. And the final problem to which study of the Rent Act calls attention is that in this case, as in others, the political public was so restricted and so ineffective as to cast doubt on the whole system's claim to be a significant form of democratic representative government.

By the 'political public' one may mean those members of the general public who are formally entitled to participate in the political life of the community, or, in this context more usefully, one may talk of the actual

[1] See A. Downs, *An Economic Theory of Democracy* (Harper & Row, 1957), on the problem of costs, especially Part III.

[2] Barnett, op. cit., p. 266.

[3] One of our major points of disagreement with W. Kornhauser's analysis in his *Politics of Mass Society* (Routledge & Kegan Paul, 1960) is therefore his implicit restriction of 'intermediary group' to the organized.

(as opposed to formal) political public to mean those members of the general public who do in fact participate, however irregularly or infrequently, in the public political life of their society. Many factors may, on any given occasion, limit the real political public to a mere section of the formal political public. For one thing, different kinds of issue tend to involve or activate different numbers and different kinds of people. The more technical the matter, for example, the more likely that the general public will be represented only, if at all, by a very small, highly specialized particular public. Other issues will tend only to mobilize certain existing organized pressure groups, and yet other issues, those which seem to touch on basic questions of the division of power and opportunity within society, will tend to mobilize those groups and individuals who belong to what we have called an interest.[1] Comparatively few issues, and those only the most dramatic and most exciting, can be expected seriously to mobilize the entire potential public within a community.

These limitations upon the actual political public may be regarded as 'tactical'. A much more serious problem is presented by those 'strategic' limitations which reflect the basic structure of society itself. This phenomenon has been most visible in the United States where some 40 million members of the formal political public are so far outside the actual one as never even to vote in presidential elections. The analyses put forward by E. E. Schattschneider[2] and W. D. Burnham[3] suggest that the reasons are threefold: poverty, the new political alignment of the 1890s, which was designed to isolate radicalism and the negro, and a consequent political predominance of middle-class values and perspectives which has served to leave those who do not share them politically apathetic or alienated in the face of a system which speaks a 'foreign language'.

In Britain the strategic limitations may not be as stark, while the Labour Party has at least tried to reach out to the socially deprived, but they exist. Unorganized labour, the chronic sick, the more poorly educated, the ill- or un-housed, and the expanding immigrant population all constitute, at best, peripheral members of the political public, and here, as in America, it remains true that 'to be poor is not itself a status which defines a common political interest'[4] capable of exercising its due

[1] For an illuminating discussion of the relationship between kinds of issue, types of actor, and the locus of decision making within the US Federal Government, see T. Lowi, 'American Business, Public Policy, Case Studies and Political Theory', *World Politics*, XVI, 1963–4, pp. 677–715.

[2] In *The Semi-Sovereign People* (Holt, Rinehart & Winston, 1960).

[3] In 'The Changing Shape of the American Political Universe', *American Political Science Review*, LIX, 1, March 1965, pp. 7–28.

[4] P. Marris and M. Rein, *Dilemmas of Social Reform. Poverty and Community Action in the United States* (Routledge & Kegan Paul, 1967), p. 185.

influence. Social and political deprivation, this is to say, tend to form a self-sustaining cycle. Whether or not one regards it as a vicious circle depends on one's concepts of substantive rationality as well as one's estimate of the danger that the excluded may suddenly intervene in politically pathological ways.[1]

'Fitness to rule'

The substantive issue just alluded to must now be faced. Why should one worry about extending the bounds of the actual political public? Are not the people rendered unfit to rule, or even to participate in ruling, by their ignorance, disinterest and irrationality? And does not much of our own argument provide evidence for rejecting at least the populist dimension of democracy as a worthy ideal? If only to prevent this mis-interpretation of the import of our discussion, some brief answers to such questions must be attempted by way of a summary conclusion.

From what we have said earlier about the various kinds of rationality, it follows that it is not necessarily a sign of voter irrationality (instru-mentally) to vote with one's spouse for the sake of domestic peace (if the latter seems sufficiently valuable), to devote little or no time to the acquisition of information, or to remain largely uninterested provided that others take care of politics in acceptable ways. At the aggregate level, furthermore, we have already suggested that individually irrational behaviour does not necessarily condemn an entire process. It is worth remarking, too, that most British voters regularly support parties and leaders who are considerably better informed, as well as actively inter-ested, and that this may indicate a higher degree of voter rationality than is suggested merely by reference to articulated answers to polls and surveys. The point is that the fitness to rule of the public must be judged by the total public response to issues and situations, it being clear that articulated opinion on particular topics may be a poor index to such other aspects of public response as involvement, voting, and future articulations of opinion.[2]

A more general riposte that might be made is to suggest that no people are fit to rule. Certainly the cases we have considered indicate failures or inadequacies at all levels, including that of ministers and the expert civil-service repositories of political rationality. Resort to govern-ment by experts or an elite is no final answer to the deficiencies of the general public, if only because politics itself is not merely a matter of

---

[1] See Burnham, op. cit., p. 28.

[2] In any case, what is politically important is never 'public opinion' per se; it is the political behaviour of the public. It has been well said by W. W. Willoughby that 'public opinion, with no governmental organs through which its powers may be enforced, is certainly not, strictly speaking, a civil power'. See his An Old Master and Other Essays, p. 287, quoted by D. Katz and others (eds), Public Opinion and Propaganda (Holt, Rinehart and Winston, 1954), p. 50.

expertise. It is, as Hannah Pitkin has said, 'a field where rationality is no guarantee of agreement. Yet, at the same time, rational arguments are sometimes relevant and agreement can sometimes be reached. . . . It is always a combination of bargaining and compromise where there are irresolute and conflicting commitments, and common deliberation about public policy, to which facts and rational arguments are relevant.'[1]

A 'rational' political system, it may therefore be suggested, is one in which various kinds of expertise, and various (conflicting) instrumental rationalities play an indispensable role. But it is also one in which the ultimate problems, those of substantive rationality (as well as those of more personal taste), are not a matter of any definable expertise. They must be resolved either by superior power, not a conspicuously rational method of settling an argument, or through a continuing discussion in which no participant has a monopoly of relevant knowledge and experience and from which, therefore, none should be excluded. In particular, the way must always be open for those shifts in the whole frame of reference of debate which, if frustrated, may lead to revolution and which most commonly are inspired by those disadvantaged or excluded by the previous order of society and thought.[2] Evidence and criteria of relevance must always be open to challenge—such being the limited nature of human understanding—and none can say what challenges or sources of challenge are improper.

Given that some people are unfit to take some decisions, but that all may be fit to contribute to others, and that the instrumental and substantive ones are not always separable, two general conclusions follow, both of which we have tried to explore. The first is that neither direct populist rule nor the unmodified rule of an elite provides a satisfactory alternative to general, if differential, participation in that dialectical interaction of institutions and purposes which constitutes representative government. The second is that 'fitness or unfitness to rule' is not so much a quality of particular individuals or particular sections of the community, as of a society operating through, and influenced by, particular political structures and processes as they are perceived by the members of that society.

---

[1] *The Concept of Representation*, p. 211.
[2] See, e.g., R. Dahrendorff, 'On the Origin of Social Inequality', in P. Laslett and G. Runciman (eds), *Philosophy, Politics and Society*, Second Series (Blackwell, 1962), pp. 88–109.

Index

GEORGE ALLEN & UNWIN LTD

Head Office
40 Museum Street, London, W.C.1
Telephone: 01-405 8577

Sales, Distribution and Accounts Departments
Park Lane, Hemel Hempstead, Herts.
Telephone: 0442 3244

Athens: 7 Stadiou Street, Athens 125
Auckland: P.O. Box 36013, Auckland 9
Barbados: P.O. Box 222, Bridgetown
Bombay: 103/5 Fort Street, Bombay 1
Calcutta: 285J Bepin Behari Ganguli Street, Calcutta 12
Dacca: Alico Building, 18 Motijheel, Dacca 2
Hong Kong: 105 Wing on Mansion, 26 Hankow Road, Kowloon
Ibadan: P.O. Box 62
Johannesburg: P.O. Box 23134, Joubert Park
Karachi: Karachi Chambers, McLeod Road, Karachi 2
Lahore: 22 Falettis' Hotel, Egerton Road
Madras: 2/18 Mount Road, Madras 2
Manila: P.O. Box 157, Quezon City, D-502
Mexico: Serapio Rendon 125, Mexico 4, D.F.
Nairobi: P.O. Box 30583
New Delhi: 1/18B Asaf Ali Road, New Delhi 1
Rio de Janeiro: Caixa Postal 2537-ZC-00
Singapore: 36c Prinsep Street, Singapore 7
Sydney N.S.W. 2000: Bradbury House, 55 York Street
Tokyo: C.P.O. Box 1728, Tokyo 100-91
Toronto: 145 Adelaide Street West, Toronto 1